Pocket **BIOGRAPHIES**

Beethoven

ANNE PIMLOTT BAKER

SUTTON PUBLISHING

First published in 1997 by
Sutton Publishing Limited · Phoenix Mill
Thrupp · Stroud · Gloucestershire · GL5 2BU

British Library Cataloguing in Publication Data
A catalogue record for this book is available from the
British Library

ISBN 0-7509-1509-9

 ALAN SUTTON™ and SUTTON™ are the
trade marks of Sutton Publishing Limited

Typeset in 13/18 pt Perpetua.
Typesetting and origination by
Sutton Publishing Limited.
Printed in Great Britain by
The Guernsey Press Company Limited,
Guernsey, Channel Islands.

CONTENTS

'To us musicians the work of Beethoven parallels the pillars of smoke and fire which led the Israelites through the desert.'

Franz Liszt, 1852

CHRONOLOGY

15 or 16 Dec. 1770	Beethoven born at 515 Bonngasse, Bonn
26 Mar. 1778	Beethoven first performs in public, in Cologne
1780	Beethoven begins lessons with Christian Gottlob Neefe
15 April 1784	Death of Elector Maximilian Friedrich
June 1784	Beethoven appointed assistant court organist to Elector of Cologne
Mar.–May 1787	Beethoven visits Vienna to study with Mozart
17 July 1787	Death of Beethoven's mother
20 Nov. 1789	Beethoven's father retires
25 Dec. 1790	Haydn visits Bonn on his way to London
Nov. 1792	Beethoven goes to Vienna to study with Haydn, and never returns
18 Dec. 1792	Death of Beethoven's father
29 Mar. 1795	Beethoven's first public performance in Vienna
Summer 1795	Publication of his three Piano Trios, op. 1
2 April 1800	Beethoven's first benefit concert in Vienna

Oct. 1802	Beethoven writes the 'Heiligenstadt Testament'
Jan. 1803	Beethoven appointed composer at Theater an der Wien
5 April 1803	Benefit concert at Theater an der Wien
April 1804	Contract at Theater an der Wien lapses
13 Nov. 1805	French occupation of Vienna
20 Nov. 1805	First performance of *Leonore* (revised as *Fidelio* 1814)
Nov. 1806	'Razumovsky' quartets completed
13 Sept. 1807	Mass in C performed at Eisenstadt
Oct. 1808	Beethoven invited to be Kapellmeister to King of Westphalia
22 Dec. 1808	Benefit concert, including Fifth and Sixth Symphonies
Mar. 1809	Annuity contract of 4,000 florins a year
11–12 May 1809	French bombardment and occupation of Vienna
31 May 1809	Death of Haydn
6–7 July 1812	'Immortal Beloved' letters
July 1812	Beethoven meets Goethe at Teplitz
8 Dec. 1813	First performance of *Wellington's Victory*
29 Nov. 1814	Gala concert before rulers of Europe
15 Nov. 1815	Death of Carl Caspar van Beethoven
8 April 1820	Court of Appeal rules in Beethoven's favour over guardianship of Karl
Jan. 1823	Beethoven accepts commission for

	three quartets from Prince Galitzin
7 May 1824	Benefit concert includes première of Ninth Symphony
6 Aug. 1826	Karl attempts suicide
2 Dec. 1826	Beethoven falls ill on journey back to Vienna from Gneixendorf
26 Mar. 1827	Death of Beethoven at his lodgings in the Schwarzspanierhaus, Vienna

ONE

A SERVANT OF THE COURT

Ludwig van Beethoven was born on 15 or 16 December 1770 in lodgings at 515 Bonngasse in Bonn, chosen as the residence of the Elector of Cologne in 1257. The Catholic Electorate of Cologne was part of the Holy Roman Empire, ruled from Vienna by the Hapsburg monarchy, and the Elector was both archbishop and secular ruler. Bonn had no industry or commerce, and existed solely as the seat of the court – it was said that 'all Bonn was fed from the Elector's kitchen' – with a population of about 9,500 in 1770. Beethoven's grandfather, Ludwig van Beethoven, came from Malines, near Antwerp, in the Austrian Netherlands; son of a master baker, he was a bass singer in the electoral chapel at Bonn from 1733 until his appointment as Kapellmeister to the Elector in 1761. As Kapell-meister he was in charge not only of the chapel choir and the music for the services, but was also responsible for the court ballroom, concert hall and theatre. He managed to find time to run a successful wine business on the side, but his wife was removed to a nunnery because of drunkenness. Beethoven idolized his grandfather, although he had died in 1773 when Beethoven was only three, and always hoped to become a Kapellmeister himself, even going so far as to give himself the title 'Royal Imperial Kapellmeister and Composer' in 1818.

Ludwig van Beethoven's only surviving child was Beethoven's father, Johann van Beethoven, born in about 1740, also a court musician in Bonn, a tenor singer and music teacher. In 1767, against his father's wishes, he married Maria Magdalena, daughter of Heinrich Keverich, overseer of the kitchen at the palace of the Elector of Trier. His father alleged that she had been a chambermaid, but there is no evidence that this was so. She was a young widow, previously married to the valet of the Elector of Trier. Beethoven was their second child: their first child, Ludwig Maria, baptised on 2 April 1769, lived for only six days. They went on to have five more children after Beethoven, but only two, Caspar Anton Carl, born in 1774, and Nikolaus Johann, born in 1776, survived infancy. The last, Maria Margaretha, died aged one, in 1787, four months after the death of her mother.

Beethoven seems to have been confused for most of his life about the year of his birth, maintaining that he was born in 1771, not 1770; after he moved to Vienna he regularly deducted two years, or sometimes more, from his age, insisting that the baptismal certificate from 17 December 1770 was that of his elder brother Ludwig Maria and that his own had either disappeared or had never existed. It has sometimes been said that Beethoven's father was responsible for falsifying his son's age in order to promote him as a child prodigy like Mozart, but it seems that Johann van Beethoven was not to blame for this, and that Beethoven himself believed his birthdate to be wrong. This is connected to another of Beethoven's fantasies, that he was of noble birth, and that his true ancestry had been concealed by Johann and Maria, who were not his real parents at all. From 1810 the rumour circulated that Beethoven was the illegitimate son of a king of Prussia (either Friedrich Wilhelm II or Frederick the Great), and this was perpetuated in music encyclopedias for the rest of his life. He never denied it. He passed as a member of the nobility in Vienna, where it was assumed, wrongly, that 'van' was the equivalent of the German 'von'.

Beethoven had a lonely and unhappy childhood. He was shy and withdrawn, with few friends, and made little progress at school, and he felt neglected and unloved. His father treated him severely, and after he began to teach him music at the age of four or five he used to force him to practise for hours. Visitors remembered the child standing in front of the piano, crying, and when his father's drinking companion, Tobias Pfeiffer, was staying in the house and giving him lessons, the young Beethoven was sometimes woken late at night for a lesson, and kept up all night at the piano. His mother does not seem to have intervened in all this. Beethoven first performed in public at a concert in Cologne in 1778, but any creativity was stifled by his father, who would not let him improvise, and he left the cathedral school at the age of ten, ready to start work as a court musician.

Beethoven had various teachers apart from his father, including the court organist, Gilles van den

Eeden, but the most important influence was Christian Gottlob Neefe, who began to teach him composition in about 1780, and later piano and figured bass. Neefe, a Protestant from Chemnitz in Saxony, and a protégé of Johann Hiller, Bach's successor as cantor of St Thomas's Church in Leipzig, came to Bonn in 1779 to join the Grossman and Helmuth theatre company, and was appointed to succeed van den Eeden as court organist in 1781. Neefe admired Bach, and used his *Well Tempered Clavier* as a basis for Beethoven's instruction. He trained Beethoven as assistant court organist, and left his twelve-year-old pupil in charge when he went away in June 1782. In 1783 Neefe used him as the harpsichordist in the court opera orchestra, conducting the orchestra from the keyboard. At the same time Beethoven was beginning to compose, and Neefe arranged for the publication of nine variations for the piano on a march by Dressler, and three piano sonatas dedicated to the Elector Maximilian Friedrich, in 1783. In his dedicatory letter for these sonatas, Beethoven wrote: 'my Muse in hours of sacred inspiration has often whispered to me – "make the attempt, just put down on paper the harmonies of your soul" . . . My Muse insisted – I obeyed and I composed.' In 1783 Neefe predicted, in Cramer's *Magazin der Musik*, that Beethoven would become a second Wolfgang Amadeus Mozart if he continued as he had begun, and after Beethoven's arrival in Vienna he wrote to Neefe thanking him for all his help: 'Should I ever become a great man, you too will have to share in my success.'[1] Ten compositions survive from the period 1782–5.

Until now Beethoven had been unpaid, but in 1784 he successfully petitioned the new Elector for an official appointment as assistant court organist, as his father, who had become a heavy drinker, was no longer able to support his family, and Beethoven's salary was fixed at 150 florins a year. An official report on the musical establishment of the court at Bonn, prepared for the new Elector, had already noted that Johann van Beethoven had a 'very stale voice' and that his son was playing the organ but received no salary. Johann had hoped to succeed his father as Kapellmeister in 1773, and survived for the next ten years thanks to the protection of Count Kaspar von Belderbusch, a friend of his father's. But von Belderbusch died in 1784, and although Johann remained on the electoral payroll, he was becoming increasingly ineffectual. His wife ran the household, frequently complaining about her drunken husband.

Between 1785 and 1789 Beethoven seems to have stopped composing, as he became more and more burdened with the financial responsibility for his family, and with coping with his alcoholic father. On one occasion he had to intercede with the police after his father was arrested for drunkenness. In 1787 the Elector sent him to Vienna, probably in order to have lessons from Mozart, but although he did play to Mozart and impressed him with his improvisation, after only two weeks he was forced to rush back to Bonn because his mother, who was suffering from tuberculosis, had taken a turn for the worse. She died in July 1787, soon after his return, and in 1789 Beethoven petitioned the Elector for half his father's salary, in addition to his own salary, so that he could support his two brothers. Although this was granted, and it was arranged that Johann van Beethoven would be retired on half pay, Beethoven never made the necessary arrangements with the Exchequer, because his father begged him not to, dreading the humiliation. Instead, his father paid him the 100 florins a year himself.

After his mother's death, Beethoven was befriended by a widow, Frau von Breuning, who had four children, one of whom, Stephan, became one of Beethoven's closest friends in Vienna. He spent a good deal of time with the von Breunings, and it was at their house that he became better acquainted with Count Ferdinand Waldstein, a close friend of the new Elector. Waldstein was his first important patron and in 1805 Beethoven dedicated his piano sonata op. 53 to him. The new Elector, Maximilian Franz, was the youngest son of the Empress Maria Theresa of Austria, and brother of the Emperor Joseph II and Marie Antoinette, wife of the French king, Louis XVI. Under his rule Bonn became a centre of the Enlightenment. By an electoral decree of 1785 Bonn Academy became a university, and the Elector supported music, literature and the theatre, while attempting to follow his brother's lead in easing political repression. Beethoven, whose education had been very rudimentary, read popularized versions of the works of the leading thinkers, including Kant, and even attended lectures at the university, and was later to identify with the ideals of the Enlightenment and the French Revolution. Although Beethoven himself was not a member, many of his friends and acquaintances, including Neefe, belonged to the *Lese-Gesellschaft* (Reading Society), founded in 1787 after the clandestine Order of Illuminati had been forced to close down; it was the *Lese-Gesellschaft* that commissioned him in 1790 to write the music for a *Cantata on the Death of the Emperor Joseph II*, an 'enlightened' ruler. The cantata, regarded by Brahms as Beethoven's first masterpiece, was not published or performed in his lifetime. It is evidence, however, that Beethoven was concerned with political freedom from an early age, and the theme of the death of the hero was to reappear in works such as the *Eroica* symphony, *Fidelio*, and the *Egmont* overture. His *Cantata on the Accession of the Emperor Leopold II*, written later in 1790, was less successful.

From 1789 Beethoven played the viola in the court chapel and theatre orchestras, and also built up a reputation as a virtuoso piano player. He started to compose again, very much in the style of Mozart, whose music was very popular in Bonn in the 1780s. Much of Beethoven's music of this period was written to entertain the court and included piano quartets, wind music, songs, and music for solo piano. He was not yet acclaimed as a composer and it is interesting that his name does not appear as a composer on a list of chapel and court musicians of the Elector of Cologne, drawn up in 1791, although by 1792 he had composed over fifty works. He was also in demand as a music teacher although he always disliked teaching. He was beginning to feel the restrictions of life in Bonn, where a musician was merely a servant of the court.

In 1790 Joseph Haydn spent a few days in Bonn on his way to London from Vienna, and again on his way back in 1792, when the court orchestra gave a concert in his honour. On one of these visits, probably the latter, Beethoven showed him some of his compositions, including the Joseph II cantata, and Haydn agreed to take him on as a pupil.

Thanks to Count Waldstein, the Elector agreed to pay for Beethoven to go to Vienna to study with Haydn. Fifteen of his friends wrote messages in an autograph album which they presented to him before his departure; Count Waldstein wrote: 'You are going to Vienna in fulfilment of your long frustrated wishes. The Genius of Mozart is mourning and weeping over the death of her pupil. . . . You shall receive Mozart's spirit from Haydn's hands.'[2] Beethoven set off in November 1792, intending to return to Bonn, perhaps as Kapellmeister, but in 1794 the Electorate was dissolved when the French armies occupied the Rhineland, and Beethoven remained in Vienna for the rest of his life.

T W O

VIENNA

Beethoven arrived in Vienna on 10 November 1792, not yet twenty-two and eager to begin composition lessons with Haydn. He found himself an attic room but he had scarcely had time to settle in before he received the news that his father had died suddenly, in Bonn, on 18 December.[1] Interestingly, Beethoven did not mention his father's death in his diary, but he wrote to the Elector pointing out that he still needed to support and educate his two young brothers, with the result that the Elector doubled his salary. These quarterly payments continued until March 1794, and his brothers were soon to follow him to Vienna, Carl[2] in 1794 and Johann[3] at the end of 1795.

Beethoven soon attracted the attention of Prince Carl Lichnowsky, and moved into his apartments as a guest, remaining there for about two years. Lichnowsky became an important patron and Beethoven often played at his Friday morning chamber music concerts. Lichnowsky retained his own string quartet, led by Ignaz Schuppanzigh, who was still a teenager when Beethoven first moved there. Several of Beethoven's compositions had their first performances there, and Beethoven later dedicated his piano sonata op. 13, the *Pathétique,* to Lichnowsky.

Beethoven began lessons with Haydn at once and these continued throughout 1793, but he seems to have found them disappointing. 'Papa' Haydn was enjoying enormous success at this time and evidently devoted very little attention to his pupil. He set Beethoven to work on counterpoint, using the standard text book, Fux's *Gradus ad Parnassum* (1725), but Beethoven complained (though not to Haydn) that he was not making any progress because Haydn was much too busy to correct the exercises properly, and it seems that for that year the composer Johann Schenk secretly helped Beethoven with the exercises, even going so far as to get Beethoven to copy out any corrections in his own hand so that Haydn would not realize what was going on. Haydn wanted Beethoven to put 'pupil of Haydn' on the title page of any works published during these early years in Vienna, but Beethoven refused, telling his friends that although he had had lessons from Haydn, he had learned nothing from him. However, Beethoven kept his grievances to himself, and accompanied Haydn to Eisenstadt, the summer residence of Prince Nikolaus Esterházy, in the summer of 1793. According to Neefe, Beethoven's former teacher in Bonn, Haydn had asked Beethoven to accompany him on his second concert tour to London, planned for 1794, but before then an embarrassing episode soured their relationship. Although the Elector of Cologne had doubled Beethoven's salary earlier in the year and was sending him an additional 500 florins a year to cover his living expenses, Beethoven still felt short of money, and he got Haydn to write to the Elector on his behalf in November 1793. Haydn pointed out that Beethoven was in debt, and had had to borrow money from him, and asked the Elector to increase Beethoven's salary. He sent copies of five composi- tions and reported that his pupil had made great progress since coming to Vienna, predicting that Beethoven would become one of the greatest com- posers in Europe. But in fact, of the five works, only one had been composed in Vienna – the others were revisions of pieces written, and performed, while he was still in Bonn. The Elector noticed this and replied coolly, 'I very much doubt that he has made any important progress in composition during his present stay, and I fear that, as in the case of his first journey to Vienna, he will bring back nothing but debts,' and suggested that Beethoven return to Bonn, since he had not composed anything new while studying with Haydn. It looks as though Beethoven had been deceiving Haydn, both about his compositions and his income, and this may well explain why he did not after all accompany Haydn to London in January 1794.

Relations between the two men remained strained for some years. There is a story that when Beethoven's three Piano Trios, op. 1, were first performed at one of Prince Lichnowsky's soirées, Haydn liked them, but advised Beethoven not to publish the third, the C minor trio, because it was too difficult for the public. Beethoven, who thought it the best, evidently believed this was because Haydn was jealous (although this is unlikely, as Beethoven was very much in Haydn's shadow as a composer at this time), and in fact the trios sold well, and Beethoven made a large profit out of them. However, he dedicated his first three piano sonatas, op. 2, to Haydn, and they were performed at Prince Lichnowsky's house in the early autumn of 1795, just after Haydn's return from England. In the following years, the two men often appeared together in concerts, with Haydn conducting and Beethoven playing the piano, as when Beethoven played his own piano concerto in B♭, op. 19, in December 1795, and although Beethoven continued to make carping remarks about Haydn in private, after his death in 1809 Beethoven talked of him in the same breath as Handel and Mozart, and in 1815 wrote in the *Tagebuch* (his journal) that 'portraits of Handel, Bach, Gluck, Mozart and Haydn are in my room . . . They can promote my capacity for endurance.'[4]

After Haydn went to England, Beethoven began to feel more secure, and began to compose new works. In Haydn's absence he had lessons with Johann Georg Albrechtsberger, Kapellmeister at St Stephan's Cathedral, and the most famous teacher of counterpoint in Vienna. It is also likely that he later had lessons in Italian song writing from Salieri.[5] But Beethoven was far more famous at this point as a virtuoso pianist than as a composer and as early as 1793 word was buzzing round Vienna that such playing had not been heard since Mozart. The virtuoso Joseph Gelinek complained that 'he is no man; he's a devil. He will play me and all of us to death. And how he improvises!' According to Joseph Mähler, writing in 1803, when Beethoven played his hands were very still, and seemed to glide over the keys, with his fingers doing the work – there was no tossing around or bending over the keyboard. Carl Czerny noticed that when he played, Beethoven's bearing was very quiet, and noble. No doubt this was the style of playing taught him by Neefe, who trained him in clavichord technique, and Beethoven himself stressed the position of the fingers in his teaching. Beethoven played in the palaces and town houses of the Viennese aristocracy, and his improvisation at the piano was renowned. His first public appearance as pianist and composer was on 29 March 1795 at the Burgtheater (the Imperial court theatre), at the first of the two annual benefit concerts for the widows and orphans of the musicians of Vienna. He performed his Piano Concerto no. 1 in C major, and the story goes that he finished the Rondo only two days before the concert, and as the piano was a semitone flat, he had to play his part in C# major, with its seven sharps.

The same year, on 22 November 1795, he made his début as an orchestral composer in Vienna, when he was commissioned to write the dances for the small ballroom in the Redoutensaal at the annual masked ball for the pension fund in aid of the Society of Artists. This was a great honour – Haydn had been asked in 1792 – and he conducted his own twelve minuets and twelve German dances. In February 1796, in the company of Prince Lichnowsky, Beethoven set off on a concert tour lasting several months, and performed in Prague, Dresden, Leipzig and Berlin; in November that year, he again left Vienna to give concerts in Pressburg (Bratislava) and Pest (Budapest). He returned to Prague in 1798.

By the end of the 1790s Beethoven was beginning to move away from composing only for the piano, although perhaps his most famous piece from this time is the piano sonata in C minor, op. 13, the *Pathétique* (this title appeared on the first edition), which was published in 1799. His first set of string quartets, op. 18, belongs to this period (they were written in 1798 and published in 1800), and his First Symphony, op. 21 in C, was first performed on 2 April 1800, when he organized a benefit concert at the Burgtheater and hired the orchestra of the

Italian Opera. This concert also included the first performance of his Septet, op. 20, which became very popular. He intended to dedicate the First Symphony to Maximilian Franz, the Elector of Cologne, who had settled near Vienna in 1800, but the Elector died in July 1801 before it was published, and it was dedicated to Baron van Swieten instead.

By 1800, therefore, Beethoven was making a comfortable living as a performer and composer. His salary from the Elector of Cologne had not been paid since March 1794, and he was relying on aristocratic patronage. But after 1795 he no longer had to support his brothers, and he was also making some money from the publication of his works, and from concerts and teaching. Although in general he disliked teaching, he had a soft spot for some of the aristocratic young ladies who came to him for lessons, and when the young countesses Josephine and Therese von Brunsvik came to Vienna from Hungary in 1799, he taught them for four or five hours a day on sixteen consecutive days, and refused any payment.[6] In 1800 Prince Lichnowsky settled an annual salary of 600 florins on him, which was to be continued until Beethoven found a permanent position paying more. But he had not settled down. He seemed incapable of staying at one address for very long, nor did he seem able to form a lasting relationship with a woman, although, according to his friend Franz Wegeler, he was always in love, and in 1795 is even supposed to have proposed marriage to Magdalena Willmann, a singer from Bonn, who had moved to Vienna. But by 1800 his increasing deafness was beginning to have a profound effect on his outlook on life.

THREE

'I LIVE ENTIRELY IN MY MUSIC'

Beethoven probably began to go deaf after what he called his 'terrible typhus' of 1797, but he tried to keep it a secret, while consulting doctors and trying various remedies, such as the application of almond oil. He was extremely anxious about its possible effect on his career as a musician, and embarrassed by its effect on his social life. In the summer of 1801 he wrote to two friends. To Franz Wegeler in Bonn he wrote that he was very busy, with more commissions than he could cope with, and publishers competing to get hold of his latest works, but he was worried about his health, and particularly about his gradual loss of hearing. He had been leading a miserable life for the previous two years because of his deafness, and had avoided human company because he found it hard to tell people that he was deaf. 'I live entirely in my music'.[1] Two days later he wrote to Karl Amenda, a more recent friend, on the same lines, expressing the anxiety that his best years would pass 'without my being able to achieve all that my talent and my strength have commanded me to do'.[2] His fear that his deafness would prevent him from realizing his artistic potential led him to contemplate taking his own life, but in the so-called 'Heiligenstadt Testament', addressed to his brothers and found among his papers after his death, which he wrote in the depths of despair in October 1802, he said that he had rejected suicide, and was resigned to his condition. He explained that his deafness was the reason why he had been withdrawing from people's company, because he found it so humiliating not being able to hear, but he did not want to tell people about it. Although tempted to kill himself, 'the only thing that held me back was my art. For indeed it seemed to me impossible to leave this world before I had produced all the works that I felt the urge to compose.' During the summer of 1802 he had spent six months in Heiligenstadt, thirteen miles outside Vienna, on the advice of one of his doctors who thought that his hearing might improve in the peace and quiet away from Vienna. But his

pupil, Ferdinand Ries (son of the leader of the Bonn
court orchestra) visited him in the summer, and
during a walk in the woods pointed out a shepherd
playing a flute made out of an elder twig. Beethoven
could not hear it, and this made him very morose.
As the winter approached he realized that his
hearing was no better, and that it was likely to get
worse, and he might end up totally deaf.

However, it was some years before this hap-
pened, and Beethoven coped with the problem to a
certain extent by giving up those aspects of his
career which were most affected by his defective
hearing. He played the piano in public less and less –
the last time he performed a concerto was in 1808,
when he gave the first performance of his Fourth
Piano Concerto – and he stopped giving piano
lessons after 1805, and wrote fewer works for the
piano. He also appeared less frequently at aristocratic soirées, and gave up plans to go on concert
tours. It could be argued that Beethoven's deafness
helped the development of his art: isolated from the
world, and unable to perform, he could devote all
his time to composing. He was already composing
less at the piano, and the first of his bound sketchbooks, in which he made detailed drafts of the

works in progress, date from 1798. In his panic, at the beginning, Beethoven may have believed himself to be deafer than he really was. In the early years of his deafness, he suffered from tinnitus (humming and buzzing in the ears), and loud noises caused him pain. In 1804 his friend Stephan von Breuning, with whom he briefly shared lodgings, wrote to Franz Wegeler about the terrible effect his gradual loss of hearing was having on Beethoven: it had caused him to distrust his friends, and he was becoming very difficult to be with. But Beethoven did not start using an ear trumpet until 1814 and his earliest Conversation Books, in which his friends wrote when he could no longer hear what they were saying, only begin in 1818.

Beethoven came back determined to persevere, and the first important work that he wrote after returning to Vienna from Heiligenstadt in October 1802 was his only oratorio, *Christ on the Mount of Olives*, op. 85, his first religious work. The libretto, with its depiction of extreme suffering and isolation, resignation to fate, and the triumph over this suffering, relates closely to his own crisis of 1802. In 1803 he wrote his most famous violin sonata , the 'Kreutzer',[3] op. 47, originally dedicated to the violinist George Bridgetower, the mulatto son of Prince Nikolaus Esterházy's page, who had given concerts in Vienna the previous year, and had become very friendly with Beethoven, but after a quarrel Beethoven changed the dedication, and gave it to the French violinist, Rodolphe Kreutzer.

During the summer of 1803 Beethoven composed one of his most famous orchestral works, the Symphony no. 3, op. 55, the *Eroica*, which he originally entitled *Bonaparte*. The inspiration for this title derived from Napoleon's expedition to Egypt in 1798, and the second movement, a funeral march, was inspired by the rumours of Nelson's death at the Battle of Aboukir Bay. To Beethoven, as to so many, Napoleon Bonaparte had seemed to embody the ideals of the French Revolution and 'enlightened' leadership, and in many homes throughout Europe portraits of Napoleon replaced even pictures of Christ. But as Napoleon's armies marched into neighbouring countries doubts crept in. As early as 1802 when Hoffmeister, Beethoven's publisher in Leipzig, suggested that Beethoven compose a sonata in celebration of Napoleon, Beethoven angrily rejected the idea because he felt that Napoleon had betrayed the Revolution in signing the Concordat with the Pope in 1801, re-establishing the Catholic religion in France. He said that while he might have composed such a work once, now everything was slipping back into the old ways. However, it seems likely that Beethoven originally wanted to dedicate the symphony to Napoleon, but because his patron, Prince Lobkowitz, wanted the rights to it, he changed his mind, and gave it the title *Bonaparte* instead. There is a well-known story that when Beethoven heard the news that Napoleon had proclaimed himself Emperor in May 1804, he tore the title page in half, in despair and rage that Napoleon was just an ordinary person after all, who would trample on the rights of man and would become a tyrant. The publisher subsequently gave it the title *Sinfonia Eroica*, although the title page also says it was written 'to celebrate the memory of a great man'. There could be a very straightforward reason for the change of title. In 1803 Beethoven was thinking of visiting Paris or even moving there permanently, and he might have thought it wise to dedicate it to Napoleon. But he changed his mind about Paris, and meanwhile war between Austria and France was imminent, and the censors were clamping down on any signs of sympathy with the French. Beethoven might well have felt that to keep 'Bonaparte' as a title or dedication would be frowned on in Vienna, and so removed the title, although on 26 August 1804 he was writing to Breitkopf and Härtel, the publishers, that 'the title of the symphony is really *Bonaparte*'. According to Baron de Trémont, a French official in Vienna during the French occupation of 1809, Beethoven continued to admire Napoleon as one who had risen from humble origins. The symphony had a mixed reception, and many people felt it was far too long. Although Beethoven refused to make any changes, when it was published in 1805 he added a note that because of its great length it should be played near the beginning of a concert before the audience got too tired.

In his letter to Karl Amenda in 1801 Beethoven said he had been busy composing all kinds of works except operas and religious works. His oratorio was written by the end of 1802, and although in the end he was only to write one opera, *Fidelio*, he often talked about writing operas, and had the opportunity, or a commission, materialized, no doubt he would have done so. Early in 1803 he was appointed composer-in-residence of the new Theater an der Wien, and the director, Emanuel Schikaneder (author of the *Magic Flute*), engaged Beethoven to write the music for his libretto, *Vestas Feuer*. Allowed to live rent-free at the theatre, he moved in there with his brother Carl; he was also to be permitted to put on benefit concerts there. Although he spent about six months, on and off, working on *Vestas Feuer*, he lost interest, complaining that the language was that of 'the mouths of our Viennese apple-women', and turned instead to J.N. Bouilly's play, *Léonore*; based on events during the Reign of Terror in France, the play told the story of the rescue of Florestan, unjustly imprisoned at the hands of the tyrant Pizarro, by his faithful wife Léonore. In some ways, the text reflects the mood of the 'Heiligenstadt Testament', as when Florestan, in his prison cell, sings: 'God, what darkness here . . . O harsh trial! Yet God's will is righteous. I'll not complain . . . In the springtime of life, happiness has fled from me . . . But I have done my duty.' French Revolutionary opera was all the rage in Vienna at that time. Cherubini's[4] *Lodoïska* was first performed in Vienna in 1802 and was such a success that Baron Braun, the deputy director of the court theatre, went off to Paris to get more. All Cherubini's post-French Revolutionary operas were put on, and these inspired Beethoven to write *Fidelio*. In February 1804 the Theater an der Wien was sold to Baron Braun and Beethoven's contract lapsed. He had to move out of the theatre, but he negotiated a new contract which would enable him to finish the opera. He worked on it all through the summer of 1805, but the first performance, on 20 November 1805 – only a week after the invasion of Vienna by Napoleon's army, following the defeat of the Austrians at Ulm – was given in front of a sparse audience, mainly French officers, as most of the music-loving public of Vienna had fled the city. The opera, *Leonore*,[5] was poorly received and Beethoven revised it during the winter. It was put on again in the spring of 1806, after people had returned to Vienna, with a new overture (now known as *Leonore* no. 3), but after only two performances Beethoven had a row with the director and withdrew his score. There was some talk of a performance in Prague in 1807 for which Beethoven wrote yet another overture (*Leonore* no. 1, op. 138), but this never took place and the opera was laid aside until 1814, when it was extensively rewritten and put on as *Fidelio*, with a fourth overture (the *Fidelio* overture).

By 1806 Beethoven had an important new patron: Count Andreas Razumovsky, Russian ambassador in Vienna since 1792, and brother-in-law of Prince Lichnowsky, was a keen violinist, who had often played second violin in Haydn's quartets. He commissioned Beethoven to write the three string quartets which became known as the 'Razumovsky Quartets', op. 59; two of them contain movements based on Russian folk tunes. In 1808 Razumovsky engaged a permanent quartet, led by Ignaz Schuppanzigh, and from then on it always gave the first performances of Beethoven's quartets. Beethoven's friendship with Razumovsky grew as his relationship with Lichnowsky cooled. This was already under strain after Lichnowsky had criticized the first version of *Leonore* and forced Beethoven to make changes, and matters came to a head in the autumn of 1806 when Beethoven stormed out of Lichnowsky's country house in Silesia after refusing to play for a group of French officers who were staying there. He supposedly went back to his lodgings in Vienna and smashed a bust of Lichnowsky which he had there, and then wrote to him that he was a prince only by accident of birth: 'there have been and will still be thousands of princes: there is only one Beethoven'.[6]

Beethoven was now a famous composer and in Vienna his works were being performed as often as those of Haydn and Mozart. Outside the Hapsburg Empire, too, his reputation was growing, and he was especially popular in England. In 1801 there were several performances of his *Septet*, and during the 1804–5 season there were ten performances in England of major works by Beethoven. He wrote variations on 'God save the King' and 'Rule Britannia' in 1803, perhaps in acknowledgment of his popularity there. He was rarely performed in France until after his death, and only one of his symphonies was played there before 1811. But despite his growing success, Beethoven was constantly anxious about money, and was always hoping for a permanent, salaried appointment. He had to depend largely on aristocratic patronage. It was difficult for him to organize concerts for his own benefit, rather than for charity, and he was only able to put on two benefit concerts in this period, in 1803 and 1808. One reliable source of income was the sale of his manuscripts to publishers, who were only too eager to get their hands on them (the system of royalties did not yet exist), and in April 1807 he signed a contract with Clementi, the London music publisher, who paid £200 for the right to publish in England the Razumovsky Quartets, the Fourth Symphony, the Fourth Piano Concerto, the Violin Concerto, and the *Coriolan* overture.

Despite his fame Beethoven's compositions were by no means always an instant success. At the beginning of 1807 Prince Nikolaus Esterházy invited Beethoven to write a mass to be performed on his wife's name day in September. It had become a tradition that a new mass would be commissioned to mark this occasion every year, and Beethoven was extremely nervous about it, as Haydn had written six of these masses in the years before 1802, and Esterházy was used to Haydn's style. Haydn had been in the habit of going to Eisenstadt, Esterházy's country estate, to conduct the performance, and so Beethoven went there in September. But many members of the orchestra and choir failed to turn up to the rehearsal, and when it was performed, Prince Esterházy did not like it; this he made quite clear at the party afterwards, when Beethoven was even under the impression that some of the guests were laughing at him. Beethoven left Eisenstadt in anger and changed the dedication of the mass to Prince Kinsky.

Notwithstanding the failure of *Leonore*, Beethoven was still interested in writing operas, and was also most anxious to secure a regular income, especially as his annuity from Prince Lichnowsky had dried up. At the end of 1807 Beethoven wrote to the directors of the Royal Imperial Court Theatres, a group of nobles that included Prince Lobkowitz and Prince Esterházy. He offered to compose one opera a year in return for an annual salary of 2,400 florins and the use of one of the theatres for an annual benefit concert, hinting that he would leave Vienna if his offer was turned down. Nothing came of this, but he did not leave. In fact 1808 proved an extra-ordinarily productive year, with the composition of his Fifth Symphony, op. 67, in C minor,[7] the Sixth Symphony, op. 68, in F (the *Pastoral*), and the Choral Fantasia, op. 80. The *Pastoral* Symphony has become the most recorded Beethoven symphony in Britain, and is the most popular of all Beethoven's works in France. Beethoven, brought up a Catholic, did not attend church but he felt the presence of God in nature. In a letter to Therese Malfatti in May 1810 he wrote: 'no one can love the country as much as I do. For surely woods, trees and rocks produce the echo which man deserves to hear.' He usually spent the summer months in one of the villages near Vienna, and composed the *Pastoral* Symphony in the summer of 1808. In the first violin part he describes it as a 'Sinfonia Pastorella', or 'Recollections of Country Life'. Each of the five movements has a title, among them 'Awakening of cheerful feelings on arriving in the country' (first movement), and 'Shepherd's song: happy, thankful feelings after the storm' (fifth movement). The music includes bird songs (the cuckoo, the nightingale, and the quail), thunder, and alphorn calls, although he described it as 'more an expression of feeling than painting', and in his sketchbook he wrote that 'anyone possessing an idea of country life can imagine the composer's intentions without the aid of titles'. Beethoven managed to organize a benefit concert in the Theater an der Wien on 22 December 1808 at which all these works – the Fifth and Sixth Symphonies and the Choral Fantasia – had their first performances, but he was very disappointed with

their reception.[8] Unfortunately the concert clashed
with the annual widows and orphans concert in the
Burgtheater, and it also lasted four hours. The
orchestra seems to have been poorly rehearsed, and
at one point in the Choral Fantasia the clarinets
came in in the wrong place, and Beethoven, who
was conducting, had to tell the orchestra to stop
and start again. This reinforced Beethoven's already
low opinion of musical standards in Vienna.

But by then, Beethoven had been offered a job. In
1807 Jérôme Bonaparte, Napoleon's youngest
brother, had been installed in Kassel as ruler of the
new kingdom of Westphalia, and in October 1808
he offered Beethoven the post of Kapellmeister at a
salary of 600 ducats (2,700 florins). Beethoven
seems to have used this offer as a bargaining counter
to secure a means of staying in Vienna without any
further financial worries, and he let it be known
that he intended to accept the position. At the
beginning of 1809 he wrote to his publishers
Breitkopf and Härtel in Leipzig, telling them that he
was being forced to leave Vienna, the only part of
the German fatherland not in French hands, and was
waiting for confirmation of his appointment. As he
no doubt intended, his friends and patrons in

Vienna, faced with the prospect of losing him, decided to act, and three of them, Prince Lobkowitz, Prince Kinsky and Archduke Rudolph,[9] reached an agreement with Beethoven. With his friend Baron Gleichenstein acting as his inter-mediary, Beethoven asked for an annual salary of 4,000 florins and the right to use the Theater an der Wien every year on Palm Sunday for a benefit con-cert; he also said that although his greatest desire was to enter into the Imperial Service one day, in the meantime the title of Imperial Kapellmeister would make him very happy.[10] The three nobles concentrated on the financial side of Beethoven's requests, and agreed to pay him 4,000 florins a year (1,800 from Prince Kinsky, 1,500 from Archduke Rudolph, and 700 from Prince Lobkowitz) for the rest of his life, or until he secured an appointment paying more than that, provided that he remained in Vienna and did not leave without their consent. In the agreement they acknowledged that Beethoven was a genius who needed to be free from financial worries so that he could continue to compose great works. Beethoven's demands for an imperial title and an annual benefit concert were not mentioned. Nevertheless from now on he would be paid to compose whatever he wanted, without any formal duties. The contract was signed on 26 February 1809.

Financially secure at last, Beethoven began to think of marriage and even wrote, not too seriously, to Gleichenstein in Freiburg, asking him to help him find a wife. Beethoven had always enjoyed the company of women and according to his friends was frequently in love, though never for long, but in 1809, at the age of thirty-eight, he was still a bachelor. If his deafness had caused him to shun the company of others, as he claimed in 1801, it did not prevent him from flirting with the many aristocratic women with whom he came into contact. In November 1801 he wrote to Franz Wegeler to say that he was now happier than when he had written to him in the summer, because he was now in love, and although he was sure that marriage could make him happy, he knew he could not marry the woman in question because of the difference in rank. But he also assured Wegeler that he did not want to marry, because 'for me there is no greater pleasure than to practise and exercise my art'. This letter probably refers to his seventeen-year-old pupil, Countess Giulietta Guicciardi, to whom he dedicated the

'Moonlight' sonata in 1802. But while she was flirting with Beethoven, she was also having an affair with Count Gallenberg, a composer of ballet music, and no doubt this contributed to Beethoven's depression in the summer of 1802. She married Gallenberg in 1803 and moved to Naples.

In January 1804 Count Deym died, leaving Beethoven's friend Josephine (formerly Brunsvik) with four small children. She suffered a nervous breakdown, and while she was recovering he began to pay her visits, giving her piano lessons; almost inevitably he fell in love with her. But once again, as with Countess Giulietta Guicciardi, she was of a higher social rank than he, and although she enjoyed his company, she wanted nothing more. Beethoven's love was at its most intense during the winter of 1804–5, and in a letter she wrote from Budapest in 1806 she asked him to love her less seriously. It had ended by the end of 1807, after which she left Vienna permanently. This was a pattern which seemed to repeat itself: Beethoven found himself attracted to women who were unattainable, either because they were already married or attached to another man, or because of their superior rank.

But Beethoven does not seem to have been

particularly attractive to women – he was in love with them, but his love was not returned. He was short and stocky, with a pock-marked face and heavy eyebrows, although many people commented on his strikingly expressive eyes. As the years passed, he became careless about his appearance, and was known to have given piano lessons in his dressing gown and nightcap. He was chronically untidy, and because he frequently quarrelled with his landladies, and found difficulty in keeping servants, he sometimes lived in extreme squalor, with dirty clothes piled on chairs and plates lying around with the remains of the previous night's supper still on them. He may have kept his boorish manners for his male friends and acquaintances but with them too his behaviour seems to have got worse, partly perhaps because of his increasing deafness and isolation. He grew more and more eccentric and bad-tempered. He refused to behave like a courtier, or observe social conventions – he would stop playing the piano if people were not paying attention – although Archduke Rudolph allowed Beethoven to ignore court etiquette when he was with him. But at the same time he followed a very disciplined working routine, rising at dawn, working all morning with lunch at two or three, and then going for a long walk, pocket sketchbook in hand in order to jot down any ideas that came to him. He rarely worked in the evenings, because of the strain on his eyes, and often spent the evening in the tavern. He enjoyed company and there are several entries in the *Tagebuch* reminding himself of this: 'every day share a meal with someone', and 'to be in company evenings and middays is uplifting'.[11]

But above all else, Beethoven was dedicated to his art and the urge to compose remained with him throughout his life. It may be that he shied away from the commitment of marriage because he knew it would interfere with his art. From a very early age he wanted to compose and, although he needed to earn a living, he wrote: 'I love my art too dearly to be activated solely by self-interest.'[12]

FOUR

'IMMORTAL BELOVED'

The year 1809 should have marked the beginning of a new phase in Beethoven's life, a blossoming of his creative powers, with his financial problems solved, and even, perhaps, marriage. But very shortly after the signing of his financial agreement with the three nobles, the political situation took a turn for the worse and on 9 April 1809 Austria declared war on France.

Despite his enthusiasm as a young man for the ideals of the French Revolution, and his lingering admiration for Napoleon, by 1809 Beethoven had become totally opposed to Napoleon and all that he stood for, and watched the triumphant progress of Napoleon's armies through Europe with horror. On 4 May, as the French forces approached the outskirts of Vienna, the Emperor's wife and family, accompanied by Archduke Rudolph, left Vienna, and by 10 May the city was surrounded. The Austrians resisted, and during the night of 11 May the French bombarded Vienna (the Imperial Court Chapel School, where the twelve-year-old Schubert was a chorister, was hit). Beethoven, unlike the nobility and most of his friends, had not left the city, and moved in with his brother Carl Caspar, spending the night in the cellar with his head buried in pillows to prevent the noise from damaging whatever hearing he had left. On 12 May the Austrians surrendered. The French troops marched into the city and Napoleon again set up his headquarters in the Schönbrunn Palace. Beethoven was very distressed by these events and in a letter to his publishers Breitkopf and Härtel at the end of July said he had composed very little since 4 May. 'The existence I had built up only a short time ago rests on shaky foundations . . . What a destructive, disorderly life I see and hear around me, nothing but drums, cannons, and human misery in every form.'[1] The death of Haydn on 31 May at his home in the suburb of Gumpendorf must also have caused Beethoven some sadness. The French troops withdrew after an armistice was agreed on 12 July, but a French civil administration remained until the peace treaty between Austria and France was signed on 14 October, and those who had fled began to move back into the city.

With the peace and return to normality, Beethoven began to think again about marriage. Dr Giovanni Malfatti, a famous Italian doctor who had settled in Vienna and who was later to treat Beethoven, had two nieces, and during the winter of 1809–10 Beethoven fell in love with the older one, Therese. (Anna, the younger daughter, married Beethoven's friend and secretary, Baron Gleichenstein, in 1811.) Doubtless the eighteen-year-old Therese was flattered by Beethoven's attentions and admired the great composer, but there is nothing to suggest that she was in love with him. It is likely that he proposed marriage to her in May 1810. He wrote to Franz Wegeler in Coblenz[2] asking him to go to Bonn to get hold of a copy of his baptismal certificate (which he would need in order to marry). In the same letter he wrote that he had had to move in society for the previous two years and but for his deafness he would be happy. He would have committed suicide long before if he had not believed that a man should not take his own life as long as he could still perform a good deed. Shortly after this he wrote to

Therese, and the tone of the letter seems to suggest that she had by then turned down his proposal. He said there had been a void inside him since she had left Vienna and even his art had not been able to help him forget it. In saying goodbye to her, he wrote: 'I would like you to have all that is good and beautiful in life. Remember me, and do so with pleasure – Forget my mad behaviour.'[3] He also wrote to Gleichenstein, at this time: 'for you, poor Beethoven, no happiness can come from outside. You must create everything for yourself in your own heart.'[4]

Later in the year, Stephan von Breuning explained to Franz Wegeler that he thought the reason why Beethoven had not written to him to thank him for sending the baptismal certificate was that his marriage plans had come to nothing. After this, for a time, Beethoven immersed himself in his work. Karl August Varnhagen von Ense, who met Beethoven in Teplitz in the summer of 1811, wrote that he seemed to live only for his art and no earthly passions could interfere with this, especially as his deafness made him unsociable and awkward in company.

While still preoccupied with Therese Malfatti, at

the end of 1809 Beethoven was commissioned to write the incidental music for a performance of Goethe's play, *Egmont*. Beethoven already knew and loved Goethe's poetry, and had written settings for several of his songs. He was to set more of Goethe's poems than of any other poet's. *Egmont* is the story of a sixteenth-century Netherlander, Count Egmont, who was executed by the Spaniards for his opposition to the tyrannical rule of the Duke of Alba, governor of the Netherlands, and whose death inspired his people to rise against Spanish domination. This theme – the triumph of freedom over tyranny – is similar to that of *Fidelio*, and coming so soon after the French occupation of Vienna was particularly topical. Beethoven spent much of the winter writing it, and the play, with Beethoven's music, was first performed on 15 June 1810 at the Burgtheater; it was a great success. In the meantime Beethoven had just met Bettina Brentano, a friend of Goethe; she had sung two of his Goethe songs and afterwards she wrote to Goethe telling him about the composer. Although Goethe replied to her suggesting that he and Beethoven meet that summer in Karlsbad, and Beethoven sent him a copy of the *Egmont* music in 1811, the two men did not meet until July 1812 in Teplitz, a spa in Bohemia, where Beethoven was spending a few weeks for the sake of his health. For about a week they met daily. In September Goethe wrote to a friend about this meeting and while acknowledging Beethoven's outstanding talent described him as a difficult person, partly because he could not hear anything. Ten years later Beethoven recalled meeting Goethe in Teplitz and remembered that although he was not as utterly deaf then as he now was, he already heard very little, and Goethe had been very patient with him. In a letter to Breitkopf and Härtel on 9 August 1812 he complained that 'Goethe delights far too much in the court atmosphere, far more than is becoming to a poet', but he continued to admire his work, and in 1823 wrote that 'the admiration, the love, and the esteem which already in my youth I cherished for the one and only immortal Goethe have persisted'.[5] He also said in 1823 that his greatest ambition was to write music for Goethe's *Faust*. Goethe was favourably impressed when he heard the *Egmont* music performed in Weimar in 1814.

Although from 1809 onwards Beethoven had more time for composition, he was actually composing less than before. However, he wrote some major works. The Fifth Piano Concerto, op. 73, later known as the 'Emperor', was completed in April 1809 and dedicated to Archduke Rudolph, though it was not performed until 1811, and he wrote the string quartet in E♭, op. 74, the 'Harp', during the summer. As well as the incidental music for *Egmont*, the year 1810 saw the composition of the string quartet in F minor, op. 95, and he was also busy on a set of forty-three Scottish folksongs for the Edinburgh publisher George Thomson.[6] His most enduring work of 1811 was the Piano Trio in B♭, op. 97, the 'Archduke'. In 1811 Beethoven was asked to write incidental music for two plays, *King Stephen* and *The Ruins of Athens*, both glorifying the Emperor, for the opening of a new theatre in Pest in Hungary, and this he composed during the summer in Teplitz. This music is rarely performed now. During 1812 he completed the Seventh and Eighth Symphonies, which were not performed until the end of 1813 and the beginning of 1814 respectively.

The summer of 1812 has received more attention from Beethoven's biographers than any other period in his life, because of the famous 'Immortal Beloved' letters; written by Beethoven to an unknown woman, they were found in a secret drawer in his wardrobe after his death, together with the 'Heiligenstadt Testament' and a portrait of Therese von Brunsvik. The letters, written over two days and probably never sent, are addressed to 'unsterbliche Geliebte' (eternally beloved), but are always referred to as the 'Immortal Beloved' letters. They are a passionate outburst, different in tone from any other letters he is known to have written. 'Can our love endure without sacrifices, without our demanding everything from one another; can you alter the fact that you are not wholly mine, that I am not wholly yours? . . . However much you love me – my love for you is even greater.' If he cannot live with her, he would prefer never to see her, and will travel abroad until he can be enfolded in her arms. His life in Vienna has been miserable: 'your love has made me both the happiest and unhappiest of mortals . . . Be calm; for only by calmly considering our lives can we achieve our purpose to live together.' He will always be faithful to her.

The letters are dated 6 and 7 July, but there is no year, and no indication as to where they were written, and this has led to endless speculation as to the woman's identity. It was not until the early part of the twentieth century that it became clear that they must have been written in 1812 to someone in Karlsbad. For the next fifty years or more the identity of the 'immortal beloved' remained a mystery, until the American scholar Maynard Solomon, after much detective work, revealed her almost certainly to be Antonie Brentano.[7]

Antonie Brentano was the daughter of Johann Melchior von Birkenstock, a diplomat and art collector with a mansion in Vienna, who arranged a marriage in 1798 between the eighteen-year-old Antonie and Franz Brentano, a rich merchant from Frankfurt, who was fifteen years older than she. They lived in Frankfurt and when Beethoven first met them they had had five children, four of whom had survived infancy. Although her husband treated her well, Antonie was lonely and unhappy in Frankfurt and she became very depressed. She missed Vienna, and various people remarked on how lonely and abstracted she seemed, while she felt that she was only appreciated as Franz's wife, and not for herself. In 1809 her father's illness brought her and her family back to Vienna, and they stayed on in the family house for three years after her father's death in October 1809 while she settled the estate and disposed of her father's art collection. Meanwhile Franz Brentano established a branch of his firm in Vienna. Beethoven spent a lot of time in their house, enjoying the music-making, and became a good friend of both Antonie and Franz, and when she was ill he visited her frequently, sitting in the antechamber and improvising at the piano. She later said that Beethoven had been the only person who could console her during her periods of illness after her father's death. In January 1811 she told her brother-in-law, Clemens Brentano, that she worshipped Beethoven, and it may be that sometime during 1811 or 1812 her admiration for the great composer turned into love. In December 1811 he composed his song *An die Geliebte* ('To the beloved'), WoO 140, a setting of a poem by J.L. Stoll which begins: 'The tears of your silent eyes, with their love-filled splendour.' Significantly, this was the only song Beethoven wrote which had an alternative accompaniment for guitar – Antonie Brentano was an accomplished guitarist. He also presented to her copies of his music with messages inside, including a copy of his Goethe songs in October 1811, inscribed 'to my excellent friend, Toni Brentano'. In June 1812 Beethoven

Beethoven's grandfather, Ludwig van Beethoven (1712–1773). Oil portrait by A. Radoux.
(By permission of the Beethoven-Haus Bonn)

Christian Gottlob Neefe,
portrait by an unknown
artist. (By permission of the
Beethoven-Haus Bonn)

Beethoven, 1801. Engraving
by Johann Neidl from a
drawing by G.E. Stainhauser
von Treuberg of 1800. (By
permission of the Beethoven-
Haus Bonn)

Beethoven, 1805. Oil painting by Isidor Neugass.
(By permission of the Beethoven-Haus Bonn)

Bronze bust of Beethoven by Franz
Klein, 1812. (By permission of the
Beethoven-Haus Bonn)

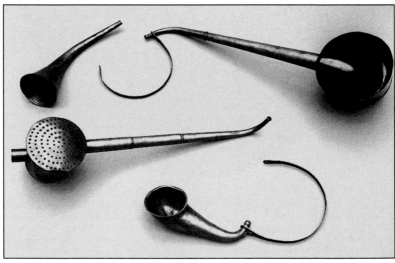

Ear trumpets made for Beethoven by Johann Mälzel, inventor of the metronome.
(By permission of the Beethoven-Haus Bonn)

Engraving of Beethoven in 1814 by Blasius Höfel, from a pencil drawing by Louis Letronne. (Sammlungen der Gesellschaft der Musikfreunde in Wien)

Anonymous miniature of Karl van Beethoven. (Bildarchiv, Österreichische Nationalbibliothek: 33.495-B)

Chalk drawing of Beethoven by Stephan Decker. (Historisches Museum der Stadt Wien)

Beethoven's study in the Schwarzpanierhaus, Vienna. Pen and ink drawing by Johann Nepomuk Hoechle, 1827. (Historisches Museum der Stadt Wien)

Beethoven's funeral procession, 29 March 1827. Watercolour by Franz Stober. (By permission of the Beethoven-Haus Bonn)

dedicated his easy Piano Trio in Bb, WoO 39, to Antonie's ten-year-old daughter Maximiliane.

Beethoven was in Prague for a few days at the beginning of July 1812, and the Brentano family arrived there on 3 July, en route for Karlsbad. He left Prague on 4 July, and began the 'Immortal Beloved' letters two days later. In his *Tagebuch*, which he started writing at the end of 1812, there is a reference to 'A', when he writes: 'for you there is no longer any happiness, except within yourself, in your art . . . Nothing at all must fetter me to life.' He also says he must submit to his fate for the sake of his art.[8]

All this is very convincing, and it seems likely that Beethoven was in love with Antonie Brentano, but had assumed they could never marry because she was already married. It may be that by the time they met in Prague she was so infatuated that she was prepared to leave her husband for Beethoven, and not go back to Frankfurt, but that Beethoven, although tempted and in great anguish, realized that it must not happen, partly because of his friendship with her husband and the impossibility of betraying him, and also because marriage might put an end to his creative powers. After the summer of 1812 he seems to have given up the idea of marriage and to have decided finally to dedicate himself solely to his art: 'Live only in your art . . . This is . . . the only existence for you'.[9] Antonie was the first, and probably the only, woman who loved him – before this, all the women he loved had not returned his love – and this seems to have been his last love affair.

Beethoven saw the Brentanos again in Karlsbad at the end of July, when they all stayed in the same guesthouse, and they moved on together to Franzensbad for several weeks. The Brentanos then returned to Vienna before moving permanently back to Frankfurt at the end of the year. Antonie's sixth and last child was born there on 8 March 1813, and it has even been suggested that Beethoven was his father. This seems unlikely. But Antonie must have been pregnant at the time Beethoven wrote the 'Immortal Beloved' letters, and if he knew this it might partly explain his anguish. Beethoven remained in touch with the Brentanos but he never visited Frankfurt and he never saw them again. Franz Brentano later lent him money, and his letters to Franz show how deeply he valued his friendship. For example, in 1817 he wrote to say how much he missed Franz's company, and that of his wife and children.[10] The Piano Sonata op. 109 was dedicated to Maximiliane Brentano in 1820 (the only friend's child to have a work dedicated to her), and Beethoven intended to dedicate the op. 110 and op. 111 sonatas to Antonie, but there was some confusion, and op. 110 appeared in Paris without a dedicatee, and op. 111 was dedicated to Archduke Rudolph. But in 1823 the Diabelli Variations, op. 120, was the first work to be formally dedicated to her.[11]

Beethoven never forgot Antonie. In the *Tagebuch* for 1816 there are references to 'T' (Antonie's nickname was 'Toni'), including the note: 'with regard to T. there is nothing else but to leave it to God, never to go there where one could do wrong out of weakness',[12] and 'be as good as possible towards T.; her devotion deserves never to be forgotten', although nothing good could come of it.[13] In 1816 he ended a letter to Ferdinand Ries by sending regards to his wife, and added: 'Unfortunately I have no wife. I have found *only one* whom no doubt I shall *never possess*.'[14] In April 1816 he was writing his song settings *An die ferne Geliebte* (To the Distant Beloved). The poems dwell on the distance between the two lovers, with no hope of reunion, but the lover feels he can reach his beloved through his songs. The text, by Alois Jeitteles, may have been written especially for Beethoven as it is unknown anywhere else, and it could be that writing this helped to reconcile him to the separation from Antonie by expressing his love for her through his music. But he also told his friend Fanny Giannatasio in 1817 that he did not know any married couple one of whom did not regret marrying, and that he himself was very glad that not one of the women he had passionately loved had become his wife. After his death, among his possessions was found a portrait miniature of Antonie Brentano on ivory.

While the Brentanos were back in Vienna, preparing for the move to Frankfurt, on 5 October 1812 Beethoven arrived in Linz, where his brother Johann had his apothecary's business. Having heard that his brother was living with a disreputable woman, Therese Obermeyer, and evidently still regarding himself as head of the family and responsible for his brothers, Beethoven went to try to put an end to the relationship. He spent over a month there, completing his Eighth Symphony, op. 93, in F, and managed to get a police order to have her removed from the house and expelled from Linz, but Johann thwarted him by marrying her on 8 November. Beethoven had further family worries when his other brother, Carl Caspar, became ill with tuberculosis during the winter and Beethoven began to give him financial help in order to support his wife and son.

Beethoven himself, despite the annuity agreement of 1809, was now having financial problems. In the aftermath of the war against France, the Viennese currency was devalued on 15 March 1811, thus reducing the value of the annuity. Although his three patrons were prepared to restore its full value, first Prince Lobkowitz, in severe financial difficulties himself, suspended his share of the payments in 1811 (and these were not restored until 1815), and then in November 1812 Prince Kinsky was thrown from his horse and died, and Beethoven had to petition his widow to settle the annuity, which was not done until the beginning of 1815. Only Archduke Rudolph continued to pay him and although he increased his payments to compensate for the depreciation, still Beethoven was forced to borrow from his friends in 1813.

After Johann van Beethoven's marriage in Linz,

Beethoven returned to Vienna. During the winter of 1812–13 and the following spring he was deeply unhappy: as well as the 'Immortal Beloved' crisis, he was also worried about his financial position and concerned about his brother's health, and he withdrew even more from society. Even his attempts to organize a concert in April failed, when he was unable to obtain permission to use the University of Vienna for the first performances of his Seventh and Eighth Symphonies. In the *Tagebuch* for 13 May 1813 Beethoven writes of his unhappiness and his longing for domesticity, prevented by his circumstances. On 27 May he wrote to Archduke Rudolph telling him he was in a state bordering on mental confusion, and his friends the Streichers, visiting him in Baden in the summer, found him in a terrible condition, both physically and mentally, and thought his state of mind at its lowest ebb for many years. The painter Blasius Höfel claimed that at Beethoven's favourite tavern other drinkers avoided his table because he was so dirty and dishevelled. During this period he composed no major works and very little else, and it seems from his sketchbooks that he was not working on anything new, either. Beethoven had sacrificed his happiness for the sake of his music, but his creativity had been stilled.

But then, in Baden, in the late summer, Beethoven had a visit from the inventor Johann Mälzel,[15] whom he had met in Teplitz the year before. Mälzel had invented the Panharmonicon, a mechanical orchestra rather like a large barrel organ, and he suggested that Beethoven write a composition for it to celebrate the Duke of Wellington's victory over Napoleon's armies at the Battle of Vittoria (21 June 1813). Mälzel hoped this would finance a trip to England. It certainly proved to be a turning-point in Beethoven's life. He began work immediately on *Wellington's Victory*, op. 91 (named the 'Battle Symphony' in the English edition of the piano arrangement), he and Mälzel having quickly decided that it would be better written for a real orchestra. It is a piece of programme music, beginning with an English bugle call and 'Rule Britannia', followed by a French bugle call and 'Marlbruck', a French marching tune (the tune of the English song, 'For he's a jolly good fellow'). The battle itself follows, with cannons, musket shots, and plenty of military and percussion instruments. As the French retreat, the French cannons die out, and the British guns get louder. The piece ends with a victory symphony based on 'God save the King'. The work, never performed today, and much ridiculed by musicologists, was an instant success in Vienna and became immensely popular. *Wellington's Victory* (later dedicated to the Prince Regent of England) was first performed at a grand charity concert in aid of wounded Austrian and Bavarian soldiers in the hall of the University of Vienna on 8 December 1813, with a number of famous musicians taking part, including Hummel who directed the percussion, Spohr, Meyerbeer and the double-bass player Domenico Dragonetti. The rest of the programme consisted of the Seventh Symphony, op. 92, in A, and two marches played by a Mechanical Trumpeter (also invented by Mälzel). The musicians seem to have regarded *Wellington's Victory* as a musical joke – and perhaps Beethoven did too. Nevertheless the concert was such a success that it was repeated on 12 December, and the two concerts made over 4,000 florins.

The year 1814 was one of enormous public success for Beethoven. On 2 January he repeated the December concerts for his own benefit, but as he had quarrelled with Mälzel over who owned the rights to the orchestral version of *Wellington's Victory*, Beethoven put it on alone, and replaced the marches played on the Mechanical Trumpeter with excerpts from *The Ruins of Athens*. In February there was another performance of *Wellington's Victory*, before an audience of several thousand, together with the first performance of the Eighth Symphony; again the concert made huge profits. For the first time Beethoven's work was reaching a mass audience and the revival of *Fidelio* in May, at the suggestion of Georg Treitschke, the manager of the Kärntnertor theatre, was one result of his new popularity. There were sixteen performances, including one for his own benefit.

In September 1814 the rulers of Europe and their entourages gathered in Vienna to work out the terms of the peace treaty following Napoleon's defeat and banishment to Elba in April. They remained in Vienna until June 1815 and the festivities surrounding the Congress of Vienna included not only balls and banquets but also gala performances (including one of *Fidelio*), and to celebrate the peace Beethoven wrote *Der glorreiche Augenblick* ('The Glorious Moment'), op. 136, a setting of a text by Alois Weissenbach, a surgeon from Salzburg, who was in Vienna for the Congress (and who was also deaf). This cantata glorifies the 'gleaming crowned heads' of Europe and celebrates this 'glorious moment' in the history of Europe, and was performed on 29 November and 2 December 1814, together with *Wellington's Victory* and the Eighth Symphony. The audience at the concert in the Redoutensaal on 29 November included the Emperor and Empress of Russia and the King of Prussia. The story is told of Beethoven conducting this performance: he crouched under the music stand for the *pianissimo* passages, grew taller at the *crescendos*, and leapt in the air when the *forte* was supposed to begin – but he was ten bars ahead of the orchestra at this point (and too deaf to hear it), and so it was still playing *pianissimo*. The audience did not appear to notice. Beethoven was presented to the monarchs by Count Razumovsky and Archduke Rudolph, and he wrote a polonaise, op. 89, in honour of the Empress of Russia. He also contributed a movement for Treitschke's *Die Gute Nachricht*, WoO 94, a work written to celebrate the defeat of Napoleon and comprising movements by several composers; it was first performed on 11 April 1814.

Beethoven made the most of his success. Of the eleven benefit concerts he put on for his own profit in Vienna in his lifetime, five were in 1814 (and the next not until 1824). He made a great deal of money but it was at the expense of his artistic standards, and the only work of any lasting value written in 1814 was his E minor piano sonata, op. 90. Although he wrote in the *Tagebuch* 'that one certainly writes nicer music as soon as one writes for the public is certain'[16], he also told Ferdinand Hiller, on his death bed, they say '*vox populi, vox dei.* I never believed it.' He was decorated with the freedom of the city of Vienna in 1815 and continued to turn out second-rate patriotic pieces during that year, including the *Namensfeier* overture, op. 115, in March in honour of the Emperor's birthday, and 'Es ist vollbracht', WoO 97, for bass, chorus and orchestra, inspired by the Battle of Waterloo, and performed several times in July 1815. After this, life in Vienna returned to normal, and public enthusiasm for these works – and Beethoven's for writing them – declined.

FIVE

KARL

The Congress of Vienna came to an end in June 1815 and Beethoven's music soon went out of fashion, to be replaced by that of Rossini, who was soon all the rage with his comic operas such as *The Italian Girl in Algiers* (1813), and *The Barber of Seville* (1816) packing the theatres. There were fewer performances of Beethoven's works, and when he conducted the Seventh Symphony at a charity concert in December 1816 the applause was very faint. He was aware of the decline in his popularity and in June 1816 told a visitor, Dr Karl von Bursy, that art was no longer held in high esteem in Vienna. August von Kloeber, who painted Beethoven's portrait in about 1818, described visiting Beethoven at Mödling, and said that one of his favourite topics of conversation was the poor taste of the Viennese aristocracy, and how he felt himself to be neglected or misunderstood by them. Many of his former patrons had died or moved away

– Prince Lichnowsky had died in 1814 and Prince Lobkowitz in 1816, while Count Razumovsky returned to Russia after his palace burned down in December 1814.

But Beethoven continued to be very popular in England. In 1815 he wrote to Sir George Smart, who had recently conducted *Wellington's Victory* in London, enclosing a list of works and asking him to find an English publisher. He also wrote to Johann Peter Salomon and Ferdinand Ries in London, and as a result the London publisher Robert Birchall bought the Seventh Symphony, the violin sonata op. 96, the 'Archduke' trio, and the piano arrangement of *Wellington's Victory*, all for £65. Then, in the summer of 1815, Charles Neate arrived in Vienna, bringing with him a commission from the Philharmonic Society of London for three concert overtures for 75 guineas. Neate spent eight months in Vienna and Baden, and formed a close friendship with Beethoven. (It was Neate who was to give the first performances in England of Beethoven's Third and Fifth piano concertos in 1820.) Neate returned to London at the beginning of 1816 with a number of manuscript copies of works for which Beethoven hoped to find an English publisher, including the violin concerto op. 61 and the string quartet op. 95, but Neate failed to interest London music publishers in them. Beethoven also gave Neate the three overtures to take back to the Philharmonic Society: the *Namensfeier* overture and the overtures to *King Stephen* and *The Ruins of Athens*, but they were not well received and only *Namensfeier* was even performed. It seems there was a misunderstanding, for the Philharmonic Society expected Beethoven to write three new overtures especially for the Society and consequently, when they received works that had already been performed in Vienna, they felt cheated and refused to pay. This led to an angry exchange of letters, with Beethoven demanding his fee, and although he admitted that these overtures were not his best work, he pointed out that they had been very popular in both Vienna and Pest.

During the summer of 1815 in Baden Beethoven composed the two cello sonatas op. 102, and completed *Calm Sea and Prosperous Voyage*, op. 112, a setting for chorus and orchestra of two poems by Goethe, but soon after his return to Vienna in the autumn his brother Caspar Carl died on 15 November, an event which was to have a profound effect on Beethoven's life, particularly on the next five years.

The older of Beethoven's two brothers, Caspar Carl had married Johanna Reiss, the daughter of an upholsterer, on 25 May 1806, and four months later their only child Karl was born. They lived in Vienna and during the French bombardment of the city in 1809 Beethoven had taken refuge with them. In 1813 Caspar Carl became ill with tuberculosis and in April 1813 he appointed Beethoven as Karl's guardian in the event of his death. Although he made a temporary recovery, he suffered a relapse and died eighteen months later. On 14 November 1815, the day before he died, he made a will making Beethoven sole guardian of Karl; later the same day he added a codicil cancelling this and making him joint guardian with Johanna. In the codicil Caspar Carl said that he had discovered that his brother wanted to take Karl away from his mother, and he did not want this to happen. He wanted Karl to remain with his mother, and hoped that his wife and his brother would be harmonious for the sake of Karl's well-being. The Landrecht of Lower Austria upheld the will, and Beethoven spent the next four and a half years trying to prove to the law courts that Johanna was unfit to be a mother, and that for the child's sake Karl should live with him.

In January 1816 Beethoven successfully used an embezzlement charge dating from 1811 – Johanna had been sentenced to one month's house arrest for stealing from her husband – and he was appointed sole guardian of the nine-year-old boy. The court allowed Johanna access to her son only when Beethoven agreed, and at the beginning of February Karl was taken away from his mother and placed in the Giannatasio Institute, a boarding school on the outskirts of Vienna, run by Cajetan Giannatasio del Rio. This was partly to keep the child out of Johanna's clutches and partly because he had no idea how to go about looking after a child in his lodgings. Beethoven wrote to Giannatasio to say that he would soon need to move Karl away from Vienna: 'there he will neither see nor hear anything more of his beastly mother',[1] and in a letter to Antonie Brentano he told her: 'I have fought a battle for the purpose of wresting a poor unhappy child from the clutches of his unworthy mother, and I have won the day – Te Deum laudamus – He is the source of many cares, but *cares which are sweet to me.*'[2] His imagination began to run riot as he tried to convince himself that Johanna, whom he referred to as the 'Queen of the Night' (an allusion to Mozart's

Magic Flute), was an evil woman, unsuited to bringing up a child, and that she should be kept away from Karl at all costs. He claimed that Johanna had poisoned her husband (until Caspar Carl's doctor was called upon to give evidence to the contrary), and he heard, or invented, a rumour that Johanna had offered herself as a prostitute at a ball in February 1816; in that month he wrote to Giannatasio: 'and to such hands are we to entrust our precious treasure even for one moment? No, certainly not.' And in May he wrote to Countess Anna Marie Erdödy that his brother's death had necessitated great efforts on his behalf to save his nephew from the influence of his depraved mother. But although he could talk like this some of the time, at other times he went out of his way to take her to see Karl or arranged meetings with her at his lodgings. Sometimes, when he was impeding her access, she would disguise herself as a man and visit the school playground in order to catch a glimpse of her child, or make secret arrangements with Beethoven's servants in order to get news of him.

Karl was to remain at the school for two years, during which time Beethoven remained in close contact. Karl visited him regularly for music lessons and Beethoven arranged for him to have piano lessons at his lodgings from Carl Czerny. Despite his protestations of love for Karl, Beethoven treated him strictly. He told Giannatasio that he had had to take Karl to task for laziness, and 'we walked along together more seriously than usual. Timidly he pressed my hand but found no response,'[3] and he admitted to Nanette Streicher, when telling her of his discovery of Karl's secret meetings with his mother, 'as I often give him a good shaking . . . he was far too frightened to confess'.[4]

Towards the end of 1816 Beethoven began to think about what he needed to do in order to remove Karl from school and have him live with him. Already, in May, he had written to Ferdinand Ries complaining about the high cost of boarding school: 'hence I shall have to start a proper household where I can have him to live with me',[5] and in the *Tagebuch* in 1817 he wrote of the importance of children being brought up at home. In the meantime, in April 1817, he moved his lodgings closer to the school. He began a lengthy correspondence with Nanette Streicher, wife of the piano manufacturer Johann Andreas Streicher, asking her advice over the care of his nephew. There are over sixty

letters from 1817 and early 1818, mainly concerned
with domestic matters such as laundry or washer-
women or cooking — he once asked her advice on
how to cook game — and endless problems over
servants. He was constantly worried about how to
run his household and look after Karl, and after the
correspondence ended he wrote: 'please soon send
us a comforting letter about the arts of cooking,
laundry, and sewing'.[6] In 1817 he persuaded
Johanna to assign half of her widow's pension to him
for Karl's education and maintenance, but after
quarrelling with her in August 1817, he got
Giannatasio to agree to restrict her visits to her son
to twice a year.

In January 1818 Beethoven engaged a house-
keeper, a housemaid and a private tutor, and on
24 January he withdrew Karl from the Giannatasio
Institute. The day before, Beethoven wrote to
Nanette Streicher that he had been mistaken in
thinking that Karl would prefer to stay at the boarding school: 'He is in good spirits and much livelier
than he used to be; and every moment he shows his
love and affection for me.'[7] He asked Giannatasio to
keep quiet about the fact that Karl was now living
with him, as he did not want the boy's mother to

know. In May, when Beethoven moved to Mödling for the summer, he arranged for Karl to have lessons in a class taught by the local priest, Father Fröhlich, but he was expelled after a month for speaking disrespectfully about his mother. Back in Vienna Karl prepared, with the help of his tutor, for the entrance examination to the Academic Gymnasium, and entered the school in November.

Once Beethoven had taken Karl into his own home, the situation became much more difficult for Johanna. Although separated from her child, at least while he was at the Giannatasio Institute she could persuade herself that he was being properly educated and looked after, without too much interference from his uncle. But now that Karl was living under the same roof as Beethoven, she resumed her efforts to get the court to return Karl to her. Her first two petitions to the Landrecht during the summer of 1818 were unsuccessful, but on 3 December Karl ran away from Beethoven's lodgings and went to his mother. Although he was returned to his uncle by the police, Johanna used this incident as evidence that Karl was unhappy in Beethoven's care, and was likely to suffer irreparable harm; this was the basis of her third petition presented to the Landrecht. In court, on 11 December 1818, Beethoven inadvertently let slip that Karl was not of noble birth,[8] and when asked for documentary proof of his own nobility, admitted he had none, but said his nobility was in his head and in his heart. This made the case ineligible for hearing in the Landrecht, which only had jurisdiction over the nobility, and it was transferred to the Magistrat, the commoners' court. Beethoven felt deeply humiliated and insulted.[9] Karl was temporarily returned to his mother and in March Matthias von Tuscher, a councillor and friend of Beethoven, was appointed his guardian while Beethoven had to surrender his guardianship.

Beethoven was devastated by this turn of events, and in his letters bitterly accused Karl of rejecting him. He called him 'callous and ungrateful', and claimed, 'My love for him is gone. – He needed my love. I do not need his.'[10] 'As long as I live he shall never see me again, for he is a monster.' But he was also convinced that Johanna was behind it and that she was causing Karl to withhold any demonstration of love, and he was determined not to give up his struggle to have charge of the child. He wrote to Joseph Bernard in July 1819 saying that he had to make Karl realize he must stop seeing such a vicious mother, 'who by means of God knows what Circean spells or curses or vows bewitches him and turns him against me'. In April he and Tuscher tried to send Karl out of the country to school in Bavaria but he was refused a passport and instead, in June, Karl was placed in Joseph Blöchlinger's school for boys, where he remained for four years.

In June Tuscher was relieved of the guardianship, and in September the court appointed as joint guardians Johanna, and Leopold Nussböck, a municipal official. Beethoven now decided to appeal against the decision of the Magistrat and in January 1820 he presented a memorandum to the Imperial and Royal Court of Appeal of Lower Austria, supporting his application to have Karl Peters, a councillor and tutor to Prince Lobkowitz's children, appointed joint guardian with himself. To strengthen his appeal, Beethoven got Archduke Rudolph to write a testimonial, in the hope that this would make the court more sympathetic. On 8 April 1820 the Court of Appeal ruled in Beethoven's favour, and a petition from Johanna to the Emperor was rejected in July 1820.

Why was Beethoven so determined to become his nephew's guardian, and why did he persist in this? There is no evidence that he had any special feelings towards the boy before Caspar Carl's death, and yet within days he was blackening Johanna van Beethoven's character and doing his utmost to remove the child from her care. At first, no doubt, he felt he was doing his duty in upholding what he believed to have been his brother's wishes before, as he saw it, Johanna forced him to add the codicil to his will. But as time went on he became very fond of Karl, and began to think of him as a son and not just as a nephew. He longed for his companionship, as a substitute for the family he did not have and never would have, someone to fill the void in his life. He had written to Karl Amenda in April 1815: 'I live almost entirely alone in this, the largest city of Germany, since I must live practically cut off from all the people whom I love or could love.' He lived alone and was lonely. He even began to think of himself as Karl's father, and wanted sole responsibility for Karl so that he could enjoy the pleasures of fatherhood. In 1816 he wrote in the *Tagebuch*, 'Regard K. as your own child,'[11] and he wrote to Countess Anna Marie Erdödy in 1816 that he was trying to work out how to have Karl closer to him, for 'What is a boarding school compared with the immediate sympathetic care of a father for his child? For I now regard myself as his father.'[12] He wrote to Johann Kanka: 'I am now the real and true father of my deceased brother's child,'[13] and to Franz Wegeler he wrote 'you are a husband and a father. So am I, but without a wife.'[14] To Karl he wrote in November 1816 that the best way to honour Caspar Carl's memory was 'for me to take his place and to be in every way a father to you'. When Karl stopped writing to his uncle, Beethoven wrote to Joseph Carl Bernard, 'so at a boarding school *a son can behave towards his father exactly as he likes, without being punished for it*'.[15] He deposited 4,000 florins at 8% interest with the publisher Steiner in 1816, and in 1819 withdrew it to buy eight Bank Shares as a legacy for Karl. He did feel guilty about taking Karl away from his mother and about the pain he was causing her, as entries in the *Tagebuch* show; for example in 1818 he wrote, 'God . . . Thou . . . knowest how it pains me to have to make somebody suffer through my good works for my dear Karl',[16] but he justified what he was doing by convincing himself that it was in Karl's best interests to be separated from such an unsuitable mother. There were many at the time who criticized him for ignoring his brother's last wishes. It has been suggested that Beethoven was in love with Johanna – she told the Magistrat this in 1819 and the rumour circulated round Vienna – but Beethoven angrily denied this in his appeal, and his behaviour towards her was hardly that of a man in love. In his memorandum to the Court of Appeal in 1820 he said he had never lost sight of his true purpose, 'to help my nephew to become a capable and intelligent, decent citizen', and 'I have cared for him as few fathers would have done'.

While Beethoven was preoccupied with his battle for custody, his health and hearing were deteriorating. By 1818 he was virtually stone deaf and could not carry on a spoken conversation. August von Kloeber, who visited Beethoven at Mödling in 1818, said that if Karl were not there to shout the words in his ear, his visitors either had to write down what they wanted to say, or use an ear trumpet.[17] When composing he banged at the piano in his desperation to hear the music he was writing. He broke strings and wore out his pianos very quickly. The composer Ludwig Spohr noticed that when Beethoven performed the 'Archduke' trio in April 1814, he pounded the keys till the strings jangled during the *forte* passages, and played the *piano* passages so softly that whole groups of tones were omitted. As early as 6 May 1810 he was complaining to the Streichers that their pianos wore out very quickly and in 1817 he asked Nanette Streicher if her husband could adjust one of his pianos so that he could hear it better. It had to be as loud as possible: 'That is absolutely necessary.'[18] In December 1817 Streicher suggested that Beethoven use an upright piano because it would be easier to fit a hearing aid. When Thomas Broadwood[19] sent him a piano from London in 1818 he was delighted with it and refused to let anyone tune it, saying that it would be spoilt. When he was lent a Graf piano in 1825 it was fitted with an extra sounding board over the strings, to which was fitted a hearing aid on Mälzel's advice.

Between 1816 and 1819 Beethoven completed very few major works. Many of his earlier compositions were published during these years but fewer new ones were written, although he spent longer working on his compositions, sketching his ideas and considering every note, often revising works right up to the date of publication. In June 1816

Dr Karl Bursy wrote that Beethoven had not been well for a long time and had composed nothing new. The song cycle *An die ferne Geliebte* ('To the Distant Beloved') op. 98 , and the Piano Sonata in A, op. 101, both date from 1816, but in 1817, ill in the winter with a 'feverish cold' and preoccupied with Karl, he wrote virtually nothing, apart from an arrangement of his Piano Trio op. 1 no. 3 for string quintet, op. 104, which someone else had begun. Entries in the *Tagebuch* show that he was thinking of travelling abroad in 1817: they include such jottings as 'something must come to pass – either a journey and for this to write the necessary works or an opera', and 'work during the summer in order to travel; only thus can you accomplish the great work for your poor nephew'.[20] He was well aware that he was not writing anything of great value, blaming this on the poor musical taste of Viennese society: 'There is no other way to save yourself except to leave here, only through this can you lift yourself to the heights of your art, whereas here you are submerged in vulgarity'.[21] He was determined to write a great work even if it meant leaving Vienna. In July 1817 he accepted a commission from the Philharmonic Society of London to compose two new symphonies for a fee of 300 guineas, and an invitation to visit England, but he was soon writing, 'I can foresee no end for all my infirmities . . . If the present state of affairs does not cease, next year I shall not be in London, but probably in my grave.'[22] It was at this point that he sketched a few ideas for the Ninth Symphony (not completed until 1824), but the trip to England did not materialize. Instead, at the end of 1817 he started work on the Piano Sonata in B♭, op. 106, the 'Hammerklavier',[23] completing it in the summer of 1818, his first major work for five years. Technically extremely difficult – there is a tradition that he composed it to compete with Hummel's sonata in F# minor, which had a reputation for being unplayable – it is Beethoven's longest piano sonata, ending with a fugue. Beethoven is said to have told his publisher that it was a sonata which would keep the pianists busy when it was played fifty years hence, and in fact Liszt was one of the first pianists to popularize it. Beethoven was disappointed with its reception and the fact that the public seemed more enthusiastic about his early works such as the *Septet*, but he was quite prepared to compromise if it meant getting the work published more easily. In March 1819 he sent a corrected copy to Ferdinand Ries in London suggesting the omission or rearrangement of some movements if it would suit the English market better. He suggested leaving out the largo and beginning with the fugue, or just publishing the first movement and the scherzo as the whole sonata. (In the end it was published complete, but in two instalments.)

Beethoven dedicated the 'Hammerklavier' sonata to Archduke Rudolph, who was about to be appointed Cardinal-Archbishop of Olmütz, in Moravia, and Beethoven had expected for many years that when he assumed his archbishopric Archduke Rudolph would appoint him as his Kapellmeister. In 1819 Beethoven began work on what was to be the *Missa Solemnis*, op. 123. He intended to finish it in time for Rudolph's enthronement on 9 March 1820 but it took him nearly four years. In 1818 he wrote in the *Tagebuch*: 'In order to write true church music go through all the ecclesiastical chants of the monks',[24] and he spent a lot of time in the library of Archduke Rudolph studying Gregorian chant and treatises on the liturgy, and immersed himself in the music of Palestrina, Handel and Bach. Beethoven was not a devout Catholic and never talked about religious matters, but he did not abandon his faith in Reason, although he retained his belief in the presence of God in nature.[25] In a letter to Streicher he wrote: 'my chief aim was to awaken and permanently instill religious feelings not only in the singers but also in the listeners,'[26] and when he was writing the *Missa Solemnis* he quoted Kant in a Conversation Book: 'the moral law within us, and the starry heavens above us'. The mass was not written in the traditional style and Beethoven himself suggested it could be performed as an oratorio. It is now regarded as one of the two greatest masses ever written (the other is Bach's B minor mass), and Beethoven himself thought it his greatest work. Nevertheless, he hoped to make money out of it. In 1822, when he was still writing the mass, he was in financial difficulties again, with the cost of Karl's education and the expenses of his legal battles to bear, and he owed the publisher Steiner 2,420 florins. At one point in 1822 he was engaged in secret negotiations with four different publishers over the rights to the mass, and then he came up with the idea of making some extra money by delaying publication for a year, and offering handwritten copies to the crowned heads of Europe at fifty gold ducats a copy. He managed to sell ten copies this way.

The *Missa Solemnis* was not the only work that Beethoven started in 1819. In March the music publisher Antonio Diabelli invited fifty Viennese composers each to write a variation on a waltz tune he had composed. In the end Beethoven wrote thirty-three variations, which were finished and published in 1823 as op. 120.[27] So although the years when Beethoven was preoccupied with gaining and keeping custody of his nephew saw few major works completed – except for the 'Hammerklavier' sonata – he was, from 1818, nevertheless sketching ideas for what were to be some of his greatest works.

THE FINAL YEARS

With Karl settled at Joseph Blöchlinger's school – he was to remain there until the summer of 1823 – and the question of his guardianship finally sorted out, Beethoven was able to turn all his attention to composing. During the final years of his life he wrote some of his finest music, including the *Missa Solemnis*, the Ninth Symphony, and the five late string quartets. But he had other worries. Once again he was anxious about his financial situation: the 1809 annuity and the interest on his bank shares were not enough for him to live on and to provide for Karl, and he devoted a lot of time to negotiating with publishers in an effort to get more of his works published, although there was often a considerable time lag between the completion of a work and its publication. His music was becoming popular again in Vienna, and in London in the 1820s there were sixty performances of his symphonies and twenty-nine of his overtures. He took advantage of this renewed popularity to bargain with publishers, as over the *Missa Solemnis* in 1822, telling his brother in July 1822 that there was a general scramble to get hold of his works. He also tried to get new works commissioned, and asked the Philharmonic Society of London in 1822 to commission a symphony. In July 1821, and again in 1822, his debts forced him to ask his now wealthy brother, Nikolaus Johann, for a loan, despite previous ill feeling over his handling of Karl. (Nikolaus Johann had sided with Johanna in 1819, and Beethoven suspected that she had suggested that he replace Beethoven as joint guardian.) However, Beethoven was anxious to restore good relations with his brother and took lodgings near him in the summer of 1822 at Oberdöbling. He wrote in May that he hoped the bond between them would not be broken again, but this attempt at reconciliation failed and after quarrelling with his brother's wife Beethoven moved out. In February 1823 he sold one of his bank shares to pay the publisher Steiner, a desperate measure as he had intended to leave the bank shares as a legacy for Karl and did not want to touch the capital. By 1823 references to money dominate his letters, and during a conversation in

April 1823 Schindler told Beethoven he must not think night and day about his debts. His lifelong ambition to secure an imperial post surfaced again in 1822, when Anton Teyber, the court composer, died. Beethoven wrote to Count Moritz Dietrichstein, director of the court theatre, applying for the post. His friends at court put in a good word for him, obtaining a promise that if he were to write a mass for the emperor he would be given the job, but Beethoven did not get round to writing the mass, although he was still talking about it in 1826, and the post remained unfilled. He was also plagued by bouts of illness, some lasting weeks. He was ill for six weeks with rheumatic fever in January 1821, and in the summer of that year he had an attack of jaundice, the first indication of the liver disease which was to lead to his death. He was planning to visit Bonn that summer but never went. For the first half of 1822 he was suffering from 'gout in the chest'. He conducted for the last time at the dress rehearsal of a revival of *Fidelio* on 3 November 1822: the orchestra broke down completely because he could not hear anything, and he was persuaded to go home, where he threw himself on the sofa and covered his face with his hands; he did not move for several hours. After 1822 he accepted that nothing could be done about his deafness and gave up searching for remedies. He began to consider foreign travel again and wrote to Ferdinand Ries in London[1] that if he recovered his health, he could accept offers from all over Europe and even North America.

Beethoven was now a famous figure in Vienna, and there are descriptions of him hurrying through the streets, stopping to write in his notebook. People would stop and stare at him in the street and children made fun of him. Beethoven was not a recluse and had a large circle of friends in Vienna, who would gather with him in a tavern in the evenings, although he no longer had any close women friends; he also received visitors from abroad, including Rossini who came in the summer of 1822. But he became increasingly absent-minded and absorbed in his work, and his friends noticed that he was sometimes still at work at midnight, and often missed meals. He seemed to be totally possessed by his music.

During the summer of 1820 Beethoven composed the piano sonata op. 109, the first of three sonatas he had agreed to write for the Berlin publisher Schlesinger. The other two, op. 110 and op. 111, his last piano sonatas, were sent to Schlesinger in early 1822. Although much of the time he was too ill to compose, in 1821 he was working mainly on the *Missa Solemnis*. In 1822 he wrote most of the Diabelli Variations, and was commissioned to write the incidental music and an overture, op. 124, for an opera, *The Consecration of the House*, based on *The Ruins of Athens*. This opera had four performances in October 1822 to celebrate the reopening of the Josephstadt Theatre, with Beethoven directing from the keyboard, his first public performance in Vienna since 1814, and Anton Schindler leading the violins. This was Beethoven's first orchestral work since the *Namensfeier* overture in 1815 and it shows the influence of Handel, named by Beethoven in 1817 as the greatest of the past composers; according to Schindler Beethoven had been talking for a long time about writing an overture in the style of Handel.

In May 1823 in Baden Beethoven began intensive work on the Ninth Symphony, and this was to occupy him until February 1824. He had made preliminary sketches for two new symphonies as early as 1817, after he had accepted the invitation to write two symphonies for the Philharmonic Society of London. He had sketched the idea for a grand symphony with a choral movement, an 'Adagio Cantique' – a *Choral Fantasia* on a larger scale – and another symphony in D minor, intending that they should appear together, just as the Seventh and Eighth Symphonies had appeared in 1813. He did not start work on this again until 1822, after his proposal to the Society had been accepted, and he was commissioned to write a symphony for 50 guineas. By now he had abandoned the idea of writing two symphonies and decided to combine his earlier ideas into one symphony in D minor, with a choral finale. The last movement of the Ninth Symphony, also known as the 'Choral' Symphony, is a cantata, a setting of Friedrich Schiller's *An die Freude* ('Ode to Joy'). Ever since he had been in Bonn, Beethoven had been thinking about setting this poem, as can be seen from a letter from a friend of Schiller's in Bonn to Charlotte Schiller[2] in 1793. The *Ode to Joy*, written in 1785, a few years before the French Revolution, and published in 1786, is an ode to brotherhood, and very much in the spirit of French revolutionary hymns and odes. (The *Ode to Joy* has now been adopted as the anthem of the

European Community.) Although the Philharmonic Society of London had commissioned the symphony, in September 1826 Beethoven dedicated it to the King of Prussia, as he wanted to dedicate it to a 'great lord'.[3] In a letter to Franz Wegeler a few months before he died, he listed all the honours he had received, and said he hoped for a decoration from the King of Prussia in gratitude for the dedication – in the end all he got was a cheap ring, described as a 'diamond ring' in the King's letter of thanks, which Beethoven sold after the court jeweller valued it at only 160 florins. A manuscript copy was sent to London, and the first London performance took place on 21 March 1825, conducted by Sir George Smart,[4] but it was not popular.

Beethoven now had two major works, the *Missa Solemnis* and the Ninth Symphony, awaiting their premieres in Vienna,[5] but he was so out of sympathy with the Viennese public and convinced that they were no longer interested in his music and preferred Rossini, that he seriously considered giving the first performances in Berlin. In February 1824, when this was first rumoured, Beethoven's friends and patrons, led by Count Moritz Lichnowsky, sent him a petition, which was also published in two Viennese papers. It pointed out that he was the most famous living composer in Vienna, that the Viennese public had been waiting ten years since the first performance of *Wellington's Victory* to hear his new works, and that he must not keep his latest masterpieces from the public but should perform them in Vienna. Beethoven was very encouraged by this and decided to have the concert in Vienna. A number of problems had to be solved: he originally wanted the concert to be held in the Theater an der Wien, with his old friend Schuppanzigh, now back in Vienna, leading the orchestra, but the orchestra of the Theater an der Wien wanted its own leader, Franz Clement, and so Beethoven switched to the Kärntnertor theatre. Then the official censor objected to the public performance of a sacred work, the *Missa Solemnis*, in a theatre. It was thanks to Count Lichnowsky's intervention with the chief of police that Beethoven was allowed to go ahead, but he was only allowed to put on three movements of the mass, billing them as 'Three Grand Hymns with Solo or Chorus Voices'. The 'Grand Musical Concert', on 7 May 1824, consisted of the overture *The Consecration of the House* (already performed in

1822), the three movements of the *Missa Solemnis*, and the Ninth Symphony. The theatre was packed and the audience enthusiastic. Beethoven did not conduct but he helped to direct by beating time and when, at the end of the scherzo movement in the Ninth Symphony, the audience broke out into applause, the contralto soloist, realizing that Beethoven was unaware of it, turned him round so that he could see the ovation. But to Beethoven's disappointment the concert made a profit of only 420 florins, and at the celebration dinner afterwards he accused the theatre management and Schindler of cheating him. Nevertheless the concert was repeated on 23 May but this time the theatre was half empty – the performance was held in the middle of a very fine day, when many people had already left Vienna for the summer – but fortunately the manager had guaranteed Beethoven 500 florins.

At the end of his life, in a surge of creativity, Beethoven wrote his last five string quartets, the only time when he concentrated on just one medium. He had composed no string quartets since 1810 but in 1822 he was thinking about writing one, as he wrote to Carl Peters, the Leipzig publisher, in June, offering to write a quartet. Shortly after this, in November, Prince Galitzin, a fine cellist, wrote from St Petersburg asking him to write one, two or three quartets. He agreed, but in 1823 was busy writing the Ninth Symphony, and did not start work on the first quartet, op. 127 in E♭, until June 1824. He completed it in January and it was first performed at a public chamber music concert in March 1825 by Schuppanzigh's quartet. It had hardly been rehearsed and Schuppanzigh did not like it, and to Beethoven's anger it was a poor performance and poorly received. But a couple of weeks later performances led by Joseph Böhm, who rehearsed under the watchful eye of Beethoven, who could detect the slightest changes in rhythm from the movements of the bows, were successful. Beethoven had begun the second of the Galitzin quartets, op. 132 in A minor, in December 1824, but he was seriously ill in the spring and did not complete it until July in Baden. The slow third movement, entitled 'Heiliger Dankgesang' ('Sacred Song of Thanksgiving to the Deity by a Convalescent'), was written to celebrate his own recovery from illness. The quartet was performed twice in September and at the dinner after the second performance Beethoven, in very good spirits, improvised at the piano for twenty minutes and talked with the guests through his Conversation Book. Beethoven began the third quartet, op. 130 in B♭, in June 1825 and completed it in November. The final movement was a seventeen-minute fugue, which many in the audience at the first performance in March 1826 found too long and difficult – a review in a Leipzig paper called it 'a sort of Chinese puzzle'. At the request of his publisher, Beethoven later replaced it with a shorter, easier final movement, and published the fugue separately as the *Grosse Fugue*, op. 133. Some people have suggested that he did this just for the extra money he could get publishing it separately, but he may have realized that it was not after all suitable as a finale for op. 130 and stood better on its own. He then went on to write two more quartets, both uncommissioned. He started on the op. 131 quartet in C# minor – which he thought was his finest – at the end of 1825 but he was prevented by illness from working on it until the spring and it was not finished until July 1826. It is unusual in that it has seven movements, all running continuously into one another. He began his last quartet, op. 135 in F in July 1826 and finished it while staying with his brother in

Gneixendorf. For a long time the late quartets were regarded as an aberration, written when Beethoven was too deaf to hear the dissonance, but now most people think these quartets are among Beethoven's finest works.

That Beethoven had been able to compose so much during the last six years of his life was because he was no longer preoccupied with his nephew, at least initially. Karl left the Blöchlinger Institute in August 1823 and spent the rest of the summer with Beethoven, acting as his secretary, before returning to Vienna in October to enter Vienna University. He lived with Beethoven in his lodgings until Easter 1825, and attended lectures on philology. Although in 1824 he said he wanted to leave the university and join the army, he remained there until April 1825, when he entered the Polytechnic Institute to study commerce, and moved out of Beethoven's lodgings into a house run by Matthias Schlemmer, a Viennese official. At this point Karl Peters, who was rarely in Vienna, was replaced as co-guardian by Dr Franz Reisser, the deputy director of the Polytechnic Institute. In the summer of 1825 Karl stayed in Vienna when Beethoven moved to Baden, and usually visited him on Sundays. That summer

Beethoven worried endlessly about Karl, wondering what he was up to, and bombarded him with letters, often several in one day, and reproached him if he did not answer them. In the letters, all addressed to 'Son' and signed 'Father', Beethoven demanded visits — 'if only I were certain that your Sundays away from me were all well spent'[6] — lectured him on the importance of hard work, accused him of extravagance, suspected him of spending his evenings with disreputable companions, and pestered him to do errands for him, while reminding him of all he had done for him, and how much it had cost him, reproaching him for his ingratitude. In May he wrote: 'It is certainly very desirable for a youth who is almost nineteen to combine the duties pertaining to his own education and advancement with those he owes to his benefactor and supporter — Why I certainly fulfilled in every way my duties to my parents.'[7] He also corresponded with Schlemmer, asking for reports on what Karl was doing and telling him not to let Karl go out at night without Beethoven's written authority. He even got Karl Holz, the second violin in Schuppanzigh's quartet, who was now acting as his secretary and became a close friend in 1825–6, to spy on Karl. When he had reason to suspect that Karl had been meeting his mother in secret he accused him of deceitful behaviour, and signed the letter 'unfortunately your father or better still, not your father'.[8] But at other times he showered Karl with affection, as in October when he wrote: 'I embrace and kiss you a thousand times, not as my prodigal son but as my newly born son.'[9] During the winter of 1825–6 Karl continued to live in Schlemmer's house although he visited his uncle most days, but as Beethoven's reproaches became more frequent he visited less. Beethoven's brother, Nikolaus Johann, told him that this was because Karl was tired of the endless rows. The Conversation Books show how Beethoven pried into how Karl spent his evenings and with whom, and constantly demanded Karl's attention. Beethoven spent a lot of time in the von Breuning household that winter and at one point told Frau von Breuning that he regretted never having married and that he longed for domestic happiness.

Beethoven decided to stay in Vienna in the summer of 1826 so that he could keep an eye on Karl. On 6 August Karl bought a pistol (Schlemmer had discovered a pistol he had bought the day before and had removed it, so Karl pawned his watch to pay for a new one), and drove to Baden. He climbed the tower of a ruined castle and shot himself twice in the head. The first bullet missed but the second grazed the bone. Karl was taken to his mother's house and from there to hospital, where he spent seven weeks. Beethoven was grief-stricken – Gerhard von Breuning said he was as unhappy as a father who had lost a son, and Schindler said he looked like a man of seventy. But Frau von Breuning said Beethoven had talked about the disgrace it had brought on him, and Beethoven told one of the surgeons that he did not really want to visit Karl because he had caused him too much annoyance and did not deserve to be visited. He wrote to Karl Holz, 'all my hopes have vanished, all my hopes of having near me someone who would resemble me at least in my better qualities'.[10] Beethoven tried very hard to find out why Karl had attempted suicide. Karl later told him that he had not done it deliberately and had not intended to cause Beethoven grief, but had been drunk when he did it; he promised never to touch a drop of wine again. But he had told the examining police magistrate that the reason he had tried to kill himself was that Beethoven tormented him too much.

The question now arose of what would happen to Karl when he was well enough to leave hospital. Beethoven was determined that he should be kept out of his mother's clutches and wrote to the magistrate asking that he make sure that Karl left the hospital only with himself or Holz, and not his mother, 'that extremely depraved person'.[11] Although in 1820 Johanna had let it be known that she did not want to see Beethoven again under any circumstances, Beethoven, evidently feeling guilty, began to give her financial help in 1822, writing to his brother: 'So long as Karl's prospects are not thereby endangered, I am glad to be as kind to her as possible,'[12] and in 1823, when she was ill, he restored the half of her pension that she had given up in 1817, although at this point Karl, who had himself fallen out with his mother after the birth of her illegitimate daughter in 1820, told Beethoven that he did not want a reconciliation between his uncle and his mother. But once Karl left school and began secretly visiting his mother, Beethoven became jealous again. Karl had already thought of joining the army and Beethoven's friends decided that army discipline would now be the best thing for him, although Beethoven disapproved of the idea of the army as a career. Stephan von Breuning, who now became Karl's guardian, arranged a cadetship for him in the regiment of Baron von Stutterheim, and in gratitude Beethoven dedicated op. 131 to Stutterheim. On 28 September Beethoven and Karl moved to Nikolaus Johann van Beethoven's country estate at Gneixendorf, near Vienna. Beethoven had always refused to go there but now his brother offered him a permanent home. They stayed until the end of November and while there Beethoven wrote his last quartet, op. 135, and a new finale for the op. 130 quartet. He also began a string quintet, WoO 62. He refused to let Karl visit his mother and the Conversation Book records that Karl asked Beethoven not to say anything more derogatory about her, as she had suffered a lot on his account, and pointing out that there was no possibility of his coming under any harmful influence as he would only see her for a short visit. The quarrels between them continued and after one of these Karl complained that after hours of rows Beethoven seemed to regard it as insolence if he could not then become jocular.

On 30 November Beethoven and Karl set off for Vienna in an open carriage and spent the night in an unheated room at an inn. Beethoven, whose health had already begun to fail at Gneixendorf, caught a chill which developed into pneumonia. He recovered from this but by now the liver disease from which he had suffered for several years became worse. Throughout December Karl was by his bedside in his lodgings in the Schwarzspanierhaus, but he had to join his regiment on 2 January 1827. Over the next three months Beethoven underwent four operations to reduce his abdominal swelling, but there was nothing more that could be done. Malfatti gave him iced punch, and when one doctor prescribed good old Rhine wine Beethoven wrote to Schotts of Mainz asking them to send some. Beethoven continued to write letters, especially to his publishers, and to talk about the future. He wrote to Sir George Smart[13] in London saying his income was so small that he could scarcely pay the rent, and asking whether Smart could put on a benefit concert for him; the Philharmonic Society immediately sent him a gift of £100. Karl wrote to him regularly, to 'my dear father', signed 'your loving son', and Beethoven was still regretting his failure to marry. According to Ferdinand Hiller, who visited him with Hummel on 13 March, he told Hummel this, and said that Hummel was lucky to have a wife to look after him. Beethoven was thrilled to receive a gift of a new forty-volume edition of Handel's works from his friend Johann Stumpff, a harp-maker in London. When he wrote on 18 March 1827 to thank the Philharmonic Society for its gift he offered to write a new symphony, for which he already had the preliminary sketches.[14] Schindler showed him a collection of Schubert's songs in manuscript, which Beethoven praised highly. According to Schindler, Beethoven then talked a lot about Schubert, expressing regret that he had not got to know his work earlier, although in fact Schubert had called at Beethoven's lodgings in 1822 to present him with a copy of his piano duet variations op. 10 (D 624), which he had dedicated to Beethoven, but he was very shy and did not visit again. A few days before he died Beethoven received the last sacrament. When the wine he had ordered from Mainz arrived, he said what are believed to be his last words: 'pity, pity, too late', before lapsing into a coma. On the afternoon of 26 March, during a snowstorm, there was a clap of thunder. Beethoven woke from his coma, lifted his arm and clenched his fist, and died at about 5.45 p.m. According to Anselm Hüttenbrenner,[15] who was there, the only other person present at Beethoven's death was Frau van Beethoven but it is unlikely that either Johanna or his brother Johann's wife were there.

Karl was Beethoven's sole heir.[16] He was to have the interest from the bank shares and hold the capital in trust. By a codicil added to the will on 23 March, after Karl's death the capital would go to his 'natural or testamentary heirs', whereas previously it was to go to any children Karl might have. This change was significant, for it now meant that if Karl died unmarried, Johanna would inherit Beethoven's estate. The estate was worth about 10,000 florins – Sir George Smart and the Philharmonic Society felt aggrieved when they learned that Beethoven had not been as penniless as he had made out.

Crowds of over 20,000 attended the funeral in St Stephan's Cathedral. The funeral oration was written by the poet Franz Grillparzer and delivered by the actor Heinrich Anschütz. Eight Kapellmeisters carried the coffin, and the funeral cortège included Schubert, Hummel and Czerny. Beethoven was buried in the village cemetery in Währing. In 1888 his remains were removed and taken, with those of Schubert, to the central cemetery in Vienna, where the two graves now stand side by side.

In 1845 a bronze memorial statue of Beethoven was erected in Bonn and in 1870, the centenary of his birth, Beethoven's birthplace became a national monument. In 1889 it was turned into a museum, and in 1927 the Beethoven Archiv, a manuscript collection and research centre, was later established next door to the Beethovenhaus. In 1902 a huge marble statue of Beethoven, naked to the waist and seated on a throne, was unveiled in Vienna. By Max Klinger, the statue[17] stood in a room decorated by Gustav Klimt with murals depicting scenes from Beethoven's compositions. At the ceremony Gustav Mahler conducted massed choirs in a performance of the *Ode to Joy*.

NOTES AND REFERENCES

CHAPTER 1

1. Before 26 October 1793. All quotations from letters to and from Beethoven are taken from *The Letters of Beethoven*, ed. Emily Anderson (1961).
2. Mozart had died in Vienna on 5 December 1791.

CHAPTER 2

1. On hearing this, the Elector remarked in a letter to the Court Marshal that 'the revenues from the liquor excise have suffered a loss'.
2. Caspar Carl van Beethoven (1774–1815) tried to earn a living as a pianist and composer, but in 1800 he got a job as a clerk in the Department of Finance.
3. Nikolaus Johann van Beethoven (1776–1848) was apprenticed to the court apothecary in Bonn. He studied pharmacy at the University of Vienna and got a job in a chemist's shop. In 1808 he bought his own business in Linz and became very wealthy, largely as a result of war profiteering during the French occupation in 1809. He retired in 1819 and bought a large estate at Gneixendorf.
4. *Tagebuch*, 43. All references to the *Tagebuch* are to the translation in Maynard Solomon, *Beethoven Essays*, copyright © 1988 by the President and Fellows of Harvard College. Reprinted by permission of Harvard University Press.
5. Antonio Salieri (1750–1825), Kapellmeister to the Imperial Court from 1788, has become famous as a sinister rival to Mozart in Peter Shaffer's play *Amadeus*. Beethoven dedicated his three Violin Sonatas, op. 12, to Salieri in 1799.

6. In May 1799 Beethoven set Goethe's 'Ich denke dein' for them, with four variations for four hands. Later in 1799 Josephine was forced by her widowed mother into a marriage with a man thirty years older than herself, Count Joseph Deym, the owner of an art museum. Beethoven remained her friend during this brief, unhappy marriage and after Deym's death in 1804 fell in love with her.

CHAPTER 3

1. 29 June 1801.

2. 1 July 1801.

3. In Tolstoy's story *The Kreutzer Sonata* (1889), the narrator, Pózdnyshev, is convinced by the expressions on the faces of his wife and her music teacher, while playing the 'Kreutzer' sonata together, that they are having an affair.

4. Luigi Cherubini (1760–1842) was an Italian who settled in Paris in 1788. He met Beethoven when he visited Vienna in 1805. Beethoven later regarded him as the greatest living composer (other than himself).

5. The original overture, played at the première in November 1805, is *Leonore* no. 2.

6. The original of this much-quoted remark is lost.

7. During the Second World War all BBC broadcasts to occupied France began with the opening of the Fifth Symphony. (In Morse Code, the letter V – for Victory – is 'dot, dot, dot, dash'.)

8. However, there was a famous review of the Fifth Symphony in the *Allgemeine Musikalische Zeitung*, published in Leipzig in July 1810, in which E.T.A. Hoffman said that Beethoven's music had the power to provide a vision of another world, inducing a feeling of foreboding and indescribable longing which was the essence of Romantic music. Beethoven's music awoke 'that endless longing which is the essence of Romanticism'.

9. Archduke Rudolph of Austria (1788–1831), youngest son of Emperor Leopold II, brother of Emperor Franz and nephew of Elector Maximilian Franz of Cologne, later became Cardinal-Archbishop of Olmütz. Beethoven taught him the piano from the age of fifteen, and he was his only composition student, starting lessons in about 1809. Archduke Rudolph and Beethoven were

devoted to each other, and Beethoven dedicated fifteen works to his pupil, including the Fourth and Fifth Piano Concertos, the 'Hammerklavier' sonata, and the 'Archduke' trio. The Piano Sonata no. 26, op. 81a, 'Les Adieux', was written to mark Rudolph's departure from Vienna, his absence and return, in 1809–10. In later years Rudolph's was the only voice that Beethoven could understand through his ear trumpet.

10. When Beethoven accepted the annuity from Prince Lichnowsky in 1800 it was on the understanding that it would be terminated when he found a suitable appointment. In 1803, in a letter to Hoffmeister and Kühnel, Beethoven expressed his regret at not having an appointment at the Imperial Court, as do all of his acquaintances (*c*. 18 September 1803).

11. *Tagebuch*, 36 and 122.

12. Letter to Breitkopf and Härtel, Leipzig, 16 July 1808.

CHAPTER 4

1. 26 July 1809.

2. 2 May 1810.

3. May 1810.

4. Spring 1810.

5. 8 February 1823.

6. George Thomson had previously asked Haydn to arrange many Scottish, Welsh and Irish national airs, which he did from 1799 to 1808. He first asked Beethoven to do some settings in 1809. Altogether Thomson was to publish 125 settings of British songs by Beethoven, composed between 1809 and 1820.

7. Maynard Solomon, *Beethoven* (1977), chap. 15.

8. *Tagebuch*, 1. It has also been suggested that this reference to 'A' is to Amalie Sebald, a singer from Berlin, who was in Teplitz at the same time as Beethoven in September 1812, and to whom he wrote several affectionate letters.

9. *Tagebuch*, 88 (1816).

10. 15 February 1817.

11. 'An die Geliebte' was written for her, but not dedicated to her.

12. *Tagebuch*, 104.

13. *Tagebuch*, 107.

14. 8 May 1816.
15. Mälzel was the inventor of the metronome, and Beethoven was the first major composer to use it. He also produced several ear trumpets for Beethoven.
16. *Tagebuch*, 16.

CHAPTER 5

1. End of January 1816.
2. 6 February 1816.
3. 14 November 1816.
4. 18 June 1818.
5. 8 May 1816.
6. 18 June 1818.
7. 23 January 1818.
8. When asked about his plans for Karl's education, Beethoven said he planned to send his nephew to the Mölkerkonvikt, but if only he were of noble birth he could go to the Theresianium (a school for the sons of the aristocracy).
9. On 27 October 1819 Beethoven wrote to the lawyer Johann Baptist Bach, suggesting that they try to make the Court of Appeal responsible for the guardianship, since he had raised his nephew into the higher class and they therefore should not have anything to do with the Magistrat: 'For only innkeepers, cobblers and tailors come under that kind of guardianship.'
10. Letter to Joseph Bernard, late July 1819.
11. *Tagebuch*, 80.
12. 13 May 1816.
13. 6 September 1816.
14. 29 September 1816.
15. Early July 1819.
16. *Tagebuch*, 160.
17. 140 Conversation Books survive, starting in 1818. They only record one side of the conversation, because Beethoven would speak in reply. Unfortunately Anton Schindler, his secretary, took possession of them after Beethoven's death and may have destroyed many of them. It is also now known that he forged some of the entries, especially for the period 1819 to 1820.

18. 7 July 1817.

19. Thomas Broadwood was head of the firm of John Broadwood & Sons, London, and he visited Vienna in 1817 and offered to send Beethoven a new six-octave piano. It was shipped to Trieste in a tin and deal case, and transported over the Alps by horses or mules along 360 miles of cart tracks. It must have been in dire need of tuning after this.

20. *Tagebuch*, 116, and 120.

21. *Tagebuch*, 119.

22. Letter to Nikolaus Zmeskall, 21 August 1817.

23. Beethoven put 'Hammerklavier' rather than 'Pianoforte' on the title pages of the piano sonatas op. 101, op. 106 and op. 109 because he decided he wanted to use the German language. It became the nickname for the op. 106 sonata.

24. *Tagebuch*, 168.

25. Beethoven quotes Kant in the *Tagebuch*, 105: 'When in the state of the world order and beauty shine forth, there is a God . . . When this order has been able to flow from universal laws of Nature, so the whole of Nature is inevitably a result of the higher wisdom.'

26. 16 September 1824.

27. The collection of variations by the other composers, including Liszt and Schubert, appeared in 1824.

CHAPTER 6

1.   20 December 1822.

2.   William Kindermann, *Beethoven* (1995), p. 14.

3.   Letter to Schotts of Mainz, 2 August 1825.

4.   In December 1824 Charles Neate had invited Beethoven to come to London to conduct, and to bring with him one new symphony and one new concerto. But although he stressed how famous Beethoven now was in England and also offered considerable sums of money, by now Beethoven was absorbed in writing his string quartets, and although he accepted at first, in March 1825 he wrote postponing the visit.

5.   The *Missa Solemnis* was first performed in St Petersburg in April 1824; it was organized by Prince Galitzin, who was one of those who subscribed to the manuscript edition of the mass.

6. 18 May 1825.

7. 18 May 1825.

8. 31 May 1825.

9. 5 October 1825.

10. 9 September 1826.

11. Letter to Ignaz von Czapka, August 1826.

12. 31 July 1822.

13. 22 February 1827.

14. Barry Cooper has reconstructed the first movement of the Tenth Symphony in E♭ from the sketches. This was published in 1988 and recorded by the London Symphony Orchestra.

15. Anselm Hüttenbrenner, a composer, first met Beethoven in 1816.

16. Karl remained in the army until 1832, when he married and got a job as a minor official in the Austrian bureaucracy in Vienna. He had five children and died in 1858.

17. This is now in the Museum der Bildenden Künste in Leipzig.

BIBLIOGRAPHY

Anderson, Emily (ed.). *The Letters of Beethoven*, 3 vols, London, Macmillan, 1961

———.'Charles Neate: A Beethoven Friendship', in W. Gerstenberg, J. LaRue and W. Rehm (eds). *Festschrift Otto Erich Deutsch*, Kassel, Bärenreiter, 1963

Arnold, Denis, and Fortune, Nigel (eds). *The Beethoven Companion*, London, Faber & Faber, 1971

Brandenburg, Sieghard. *Ludwig van Beethoven. Briefwechsel Gesamtausgabe*, 8 vols, München, G. Henle, 1996/7

Cooper, Barry (ed.). *The Beethoven Compendium. A Guide to Beethoven's Life and Music*, London, Thames & Hudson, 1991

———. *Beethoven and the Creative Process*, Oxford, Clarendon Press, 1990

Cooper, Martin. *Beethoven, The Last Decade 1817–1827*, Oxford, Oxford University Press, 1970, revised 1985

Forbes, Elliott (ed.). *Thayer's Life of Beethoven*, 2 vols, Princeton, Princeton University Press, 1964

Johnson, D., Tyson, A. and Winter, R. *The Beethoven Sketchbooks: History, Reconstruction, Inventory*, ed. Douglas Johnson, Oxford, Clarendon Press, 1985

Kerman, Joseph, and Tyson, Alan. *The New Grove Beethoven*, London, Macmillan, 1983

Kindermann, William. *Beethoven*, Oxford, Oxford University Press, 1995

Bibliography

Kinsky, Georg & Halm, Hans. *Das Werk Beethovens. Thematisch-bibliographisches Werkverzeichnis seiner sämtlichen vollendeten Kompositionen*, München, G. Henle, 1955

Landon, H.C. Robbins. *Beethoven. His Life, Work, and World*, London, Thames & Hudson, 1992

Matthews, Denis. *Beethoven* (Master Musicians Series), London, Dent, 1985

Solomon, Maynard. *Beethoven*, London, Cassell, 1977

——. *Beethoven Essays*, Cambridge, Mass., Harvard University Press, 1988. (This includes a translation of the *Tagebuch*.)

Sonneck, O.G. (ed.). *Beethoven. Impressions by his Contemporaries*, New York, Dover Publications, 1967. (Originally published in 1926.)

Wolf, Stefan. *Beethovens Neffenkonflikt. Eine psychologisch-biographische Studie*, München, G. Henle, 1995.

POCKET BIOGRAPHIES

This series looks at the lives of those who have played a significant part in our history – from musicians to explorers, from scientists to entertainers, from writers to philosophers, from politicians to monarchs throughout the world. Concise and highly readable, with black and white plates, chronology and bibliography, these books will appeal to students and general readers alike.

Available

Mao Zedong
Delia Davin

Scott of the Antarctic
Michael De-la-Noy

Alexander the Great
E.E. Rice

Sigmund Freud
Stephen Wilson

Marilyn Monroe
Sheridan Morley and
Ruth Leon

Rasputin
Harold Shukman

Jane Austen
Helen Lefroy

POCKET BIOGRAPHIES

Forthcoming

Marie and Pierre Curie
John Senior

Ellen Terry
Moira Shearer

David Livingstone
Christine Nicholls

Margot Fonteyn
Alistair Macauley

Winston Churchill
Robert Blake

Abraham Lincoln
H.G. Pitt

Charles Dickens
Catherine Peters

Enid Blyton
George Greenfield